The Life Of Moses

Bedell, Gregory T. (Gregory Townsend),
1793-1834, American Sunday-School Union

Deposited.
        Dec: 27. 1832

N.º 366.

Engraved by J. B. Longacre

MOSES.

American Sunday School Union

THE

LIFE OF MOSES.

BY G. T. BEDELL, D. D.
RECTOR OF ST. ANDREW'S CHURCH, PHILADELPHIA.

WRITTEN FOR THE AMERICAN S. UNION, AND REVISED
BY THE COMMITTEE OF PUBLICATION.

AMERICAN SUNDAY–SCHOOL UNION.

PHILADELPHIA:

NO. 146 CHESTNUT STREET.

1832.

STEREOTYPED BY L. JOHNSON.

PREFACE.

THE object of the writer of the Life of Moses, has been to maintain a perfectly strict fidelity to the sacred narrative; and this he has reason to believe he has accomplished in great degree. He believes that there is no single incident in the Life of Moses which has not received appropriate consideration; and he has endeavoured to weave into the texture of the narrative all such collateral information and practical suggestion as seemed suited to the character of the readers for whose benefit it was designed. The chief difficulty which the writer has experienced, has been to bring the whole within any thing like a moderate compass. Could he have consulted his inclination, and made the work embrace a complete history of the Jewish people under the administration of Moses, it would have

3

made at least three volumes of the size of the
present, and then have embraced very many
topics which are already treated of in the pub-
lications of the American Sunday School
Union, especially in the " Biblical Antiquities." The author now commits the work
to the public, with the prayer that it may be
among the means of instructing and interesting a class of readers, viz. the young, in whose
welfare he always has felt, and always hopes
to feel, a deep and lively concern.

Philada., Aug. 9th, 1832.

THE

LIFE OF MOSES.

CHAPTER I.

Preliminary Remarks.—Countries connected with the History of Moses.

THERE is nothing more pleasant, and there is scarcely any thing more useful, than to ascertain every thing which we can about the great men who lived upon the earth a long while before we were born. It is pleasant, because it brings before our minds a great many curious things as to the manners and customs of other people, and their habits of thinking and acting in many instances so different from our own. It is also very useful, because we may learn from their example. If they were good men we shall be benefited by observing the path they pursued, and if they were bad we shall be taught to avoid their evil courses. God's holy book, the Bible, has many instances of both kinds of men; and the apostle Paul tells us, that " whatsoever things were written aforetime were written for our learning."

A 2   5

Among the greatest men who lived in old
times, was MOSES, the subject of this present
history.   He was one of the most extraordinary characters of which we read in any
book ; and he lived in a very extraordinary
period, and in an extraordinary country.   From
his very infancy he was the subject of the
most remarkable providences of God ; and
through every year of his life, even to his
death, every thing about him was remarkable.
All this we shall show our readers in the
course of this narrative ; and we hope that we
shall be able to make a very interesting and
useful book, because every thing we shall
state about MOSES will be strictly TRUE.   We
shall gather it all out of the Bible, which is
God's holy book, and therefore must be true.
There will be a great many curious and valuable things which we shall collect from other
sources, in order to explain and illustrate the
history ; but for what we say of Moses we
mean to take the Bible as our sole authority,
and not to write one syllable which is contrary to any thing there said.

But before we enter into the history of Moses, our readers, no doubt, will wish to know
something about those countries with which
his history is principally connected.   The
whole of the life of Moses was spent in Egypt
and Arabia.   He never was in the Holy Land,
or Palestine.

EGYPT, is a country in that great division

of the earth called Africa—one of the five
great divisions of the globe.   Africa is bounded on the north by the Mediterranean Sea, on
the east by Asia, the Red Sea, and the Indian
Ocean, and on the west by the Southern and
Atlantic Oceans   Egypt lies in North Africa:
it is bounded on the north by the Mediterranean Sea, on the east by the Red Sea and
Arabia, on the south by what is now called
Nubia, and on the west by Barca and a great
desert.   It contains about 200,000 square
miles, though only about 17,000, that is $\frac{1}{12}$, is
capable of cultivation.   Egypt may be said to
consist of one great valley, through which
runs the river Nile, one of the most remarkable rivers in the world : no one has yet been
able to find out where it rises.   This river
annually overflows its banks, which is the
method God has provided to furnish the
country on its borders with water, as little or
no rain falls there.

The land of Goshen, as far as we can ascertain, was situated on the most eastern
branch of the river Nile, and either bordered
on, or came very near to the Mediterranean
Sea; north-east of it there was the desert of
Shur, which was a part of Arabia Petrea;
and then, still farther to the north-east, the
land of Canaán. The river Nile did not
usually overflow its bank, in all of that part
which is called in Scripture Goshen, consequently it was very favourable to the Israel-

ites as pasture land for their cattle ; and is on that account called " the best of the land."

The only other country connected with the history of Moses is ARABIA, or rather that division of Arabia called *Arabia Petræ*, or the Stony Arabia. It is a country distinguished principally by the wanderings of the children of Israel, and will require some attention as we go along.

CHAPTER II.

Brief Notice of the History of Jacob and his children.

EVERY person who has been in the habit of reading the Scriptures must be acquainted with the history of Joseph. It is one of the most beautiful and touching narratives which is any where to be found, and illustrates, in a very remarkable manner, the dealings of God's providence. We can only say a few words about this history to prepare our way. By the cruelty of his brethren, Joseph was sold to some merchants who were descendants of Ishmael, therefore called Ishmaelites. They were on their way from Gilead to Egypt, bearing spicery and balm, which they traded away either for money, or for some of the luxuries of that land. These merchants sold Joseph to one of the great men of the nation, Potiphar, captain of the king's guard. Here Joseph conducted himself with the most exemplary propriety; so, that his master loved him, and at length made him steward of his household, which was the most honourable station to which a servant could be advanced. But there is no situation which is not surrounded with dangers. The wife of Potiphar wished Joseph to be unfaithful to his master, and because he would not yield to a wicked act, she became offended, and determined on his ruin. She framed a very plausible story, every word of which was false, and thus made her husband so angry with Joseph that he put him into prison. But the very same Providence which first led him to be sold into the family of Potiphar, watched over him for good in the prison where he was cast. Here he again conducted himself with perfect propriety, and was soon, though a prisoner, made a kind of inferior officer, and enjoyed a comparative degree of comfort. It was while in prison that God enabled him to give a true interpretation to two dreams—those of the chief butler and chief baker, who were his fellow-prisoners. Every one must remember the story of the chief butler's ingratitude, who when he was released forgot Joseph. This is the way of the world. We are anxious for the services of others when we are in distress, but think no more about them when our affliction is over; and, worse than all, when we are afflicted we are willing to resort to God, and make many pious resolutions, but when our troubles pass away, our vows are forgotten. Such ingratitude to God is dreadful.

But though man forgets, God remembers. It so happened, by the will of God, that the king of Egypt had a dream, which was prophetic of the state of the country for some years to come. As no one could give the interpretation, then the chief butler remembered Joseph. He was sent for; and his interpretation was so wonderful, and his advice so judicious, that the king thought there was no one in the land of Egypt more competent than he to manage his affairs in the difficult emergency which was coming. In this the king was wise; for Joseph had the living God to counsel and direct him.

Under the administration of Joseph, every thing was done to prevent the dreadful effects of the famine which was coming. Ample provision was laid up in stores during the seven years of plenty; so that when the famine came on there was no danger to be apprehended.

This famine came at the time which had been specified; and it raged not only in Egypt, but in Canaan, where Jacob lived. Much distressed for want of food, Jacob heard that there was plenty of corn in Egypt, and he sent his sons to buy. We cannot give even an outline of the interesting circumstances which took place. Suffice it to say, after a while, Joseph made himself known to his brethren; and as there were to be several years of famine, he determined with true filial piety to have his old father near him, so that he could supply his wants, and be a comfort to him in his declining days. How beautiful is filial piety, and how remarkably esteemed in the sight of God. " Honour thy father and thy mother, that thy days may be long in the land which the Lord thy God giveth thee," and this, which is the fifth commandment, is called by the apostle Paul, by way of distinction, the " commandment with promise." According to the wishes of Joseph, Jacob left Canaan, and travelled down to Egypt, where, as before stated, he and his family were quietly put in possession of the land of Goshen.

Jacob lived in the land of Egypt seventeen years. "And it came to pass after these things, that one told Joseph, Behold, thy father is sick."—*Gen.* xlvii. 28. He then hastened down to Goshen, and arrived just in time to receive his father's benediction, and to close his eyes. Thus died Jacob, at the age of 147 years; and his body was taken back to Canaan, and buried in the cave of Machpelah, the family burying ground.

Joseph and his brethren then returned to Egypt. As might have been expected, they were afraid, that now as their father was dead Joseph would revenge himself for their ill treatment. But they were mistaken. Joseph feared God; and he assured his brethren that he had no thought of any thing but kindness. He told them, that though they had treated him ill, God made it turn out for good; as by this means their lives were saved from famine. Joseph lived to the age of 110 years, when he died. By his own order he was not to be buried in Egypt; but taken to Canaan as soon as in the providence of God they should inherit the land promised to Abraham and Isaac and Jacob. The body of Joseph was embalmed, so that it would be preserved; it was then put into a coffin, and kept sacredly till the period which he had alluded to arrived.

CHAPTER III.

History of the children of Jacob, after the death of their father.—Dreadful cruelty of Pharaoh.—Birth of Moses.

FROM the period of the death of Joseph, during a space of about 64 years, the sacred history does not give us any definite information. " It did now fall in with the plan of Moses, to describe minutely the manner in which the descendants of the patriarch Jacob spent their time in the land of Goshen. But we may readily believe, that as long as a sense of the benefits which their land had received from Joseph continued fresh in the minds of the Egyptian monarchs, his relations would at least receive equitable treatment at their hands. No truth, however, stands better attested, than that he who confers benefits upon a people at large, need not look for any lasting return of gratitude; and that which occurs every day, among the polished nations of Europe, was not unlikely to happen in a more rude and remote age of the world."*

It would appear that the apprehensions of the Egyptians were excited, lest, on account of the immense increase of the Israelites, as they were called, they might eventually take possession of the whole land. If we examine the early history of Egypt, we shall not be surprised at this, for the country had once before been subdued by a people of a pastoral character, not more than 300 years before the time of Joseph ; and it was not until after a struggle of about 30 years, that these people were driven off into Palestine, where they afterwards became known as the Philistines. It is evident, from the whole history, that the Egyptians were afraid the children of Israel

* History of the Bible, by Rev. G. R. Gleg.

B

would eventually turn to be their enemies;
and this was the great motive which gave rise
to their cruel conduct. The history tells us,
that the children of Israel " increased abun-
dantly and multiplied, and waxed exceeding
mighty." And then, as if in the most perfectly
rational way of accounting for the difficulties
which occurred, the history tells us, that
" there arose another king who knew not
Joseph." He thought of nothing but the
difficulties in which he and his people might
possibly be involved; and the following speech
shows the views and policy which he entertained :—" Behold," says he, " the people of the children of Israel, are more and
mightier than we; come on, let us deal wisely
with them, lest they multiply, and it come to
pass that when there falleth out any war, they
join also unto our enemies, and fight against
us, and so get them up out of the land." They
had some reason to be afraid, for there was
no kind of natural tie or connection between
the Egyptians and the children of Israel—
their habits were different, their occupations
were different, and their religions were entirely unlike each other. One was the most
gross and stupid idolatry; the other the worship of the only living and true God. But
the Egyptian king totally mistook his true
policy, and yet there can be no doubt that
it was a case which required very peculiarly
judicious management. But what could

be expected from those who had no true
knowledge of God, and consequently no proper sense of justice and equity. The king
and the people of Egypt supposed that there
was no way of getting out of the embarrass-
ment, and securing their own safety, but by
devising some plan by which the Israelites
might either be at once exterminated, or their
increase entirely prevented. They did not
dare to try the first plan, for the Israelites
were too many. But what they were afraid
to try by force, they sought to accomplish by
stratagem. The history is exceedingly brief,
and we are not, therefore, able to tell the preparatory steps which were taken. All we
know is, that the first plan of the king which
is recorded, was to reduce the Israelites to a
state of slavery, and to employ them on the
public works. All the time they were so engaged they were to be treated with the greatest rigour; made to work beyond their strength.
They were employed, we are told, in building treasure cities, and two of these cities are
named, Pithom and Raamses. The sacred
history is remarkably strong in the language
which it uses to represent their wretched condition : " And the Egyptians made the children of Israel to serve with rigour : and they
made their lives bitter with hard bondage, in
mortar, and in brick, and in all manner of
service in the field : all their service, wherein
they made them serve, *was* with rigour."—

Exod. i. 13, 14.   All this was done, no doubt, under the expectation that multitudes of them would perish under the tremendous rigor of their servitude ; and probably this would have been the case, had they not been under the peculiar protection of the Most High, and by him intended to be preserved.   In consequence of this we are told, that the more the Egyptians afflicted them, the more they multiplied and grew.

Disappointed in this plan, Pharaoh tried another.   He ordered the Egyptian midwives to put every male child to death as soon as it was born ; but God touched their hearts, and instead of obeying, they evaded the order of the king.   Determined, however, not to have his purpose defeated, he gave strict orders to all his people, that whenever they should ascertain that a male child was born, they were to put it to death under pain of his displeasure.

How many perished under the sanguinary orders of this Egyptian Herod, the history does not tell us.   We have reason to believe the numbers were great, because God made on the Egyptians so terrible a retribution as to slay all their first born.   Be this as it may, however, it is not easy to imagine the distress which this order must have occasioned, or how many fathers and mothers were compelled to see their dear little children torn from their arms and thrown into the Nile, where they would be devoured by the fishes and the crocodiles. How thankful ought every young reader to be that he lives in an age and country, where the religion of the blessed Jesus prevents all such outrages upon the feelings and the rights of humanity.

It was in that most distressing posture of affairs, the history of which has been briefly given, when the subject of our biography came into being. There was a certain man of the tribe of Levi named Amram ;—the tribe of Levi were so called because they were the descendants of Levi, the third son of Jacob, by his first wife Leah. This Amram had been married a good while before, to a woman of the same tribe, named Jochebed; and at the time when this dreadful order was given had two children living; one was a daughter, named Miriam, and the other was a son, named Aaron. As is generally supposed, it was two or three years after the last cruel order of the king, that the wife of Amram had another child, which proved to be a boy. It appears from several passages of Scripture, *Exod.* ii. 2, *Acts* vii. 20, *Heb.* xi. 23, that this child was of very remarkable beauty of features, and elegance of form. As was perfectly natural, his poor mother tried to hide his birth as long as she was able; and she succeeded in concealing him for three months. But when she could not longer hide him, she had nothing else to do than either to give him up to the executioner, or to expose him herself to be swept away by the river. What a dreadful alternative. In this predicament she chose the latter course, preferring to trust his life to the protection of God, and thus run the risk of his preservation, to the dreadful certainty of his destruction if she gave him up to the servants of the king. Her conduct in this is to be viewed in no ordinary light, for Paul tells us, in the 11th chapter of the epistle to the Hebrews, that she was actuated by a principle of faith. An impression was wrought upon her mind that he would be saved; and she took the means which she supposed most likely to accomplish her desires. The event was according to her anticipations, and the interesting incident with which we shall commence the next chapter, brings us to the more particular history of Moses.

CHAPTER IV.

Perils of Moses's Infancy.—Wonderful preservation and remarkable elevation.

[From before Christ 1571 down to 1531]

THIS little boy who was born during this most disastrous period of the Israelitish history, was destined, in the providence of God, to pass through the most remarkable vicissitudes. His very infancy was encompassed by dangers, which nothing but the most marked interpositions of divine Providence could possibly have averted. For three months after his birth his mother contrived either to conceal the fact, or to conceal him from the investigations made by the people, or the officers of Pharaoh. And it is more than intimated by the apostle Paul, that it was at great personal risk; for he tells us, as an evidence of her *faith*, that " she was not afraid of the king's commandment;" which seems to be tolerably decisive evidence, that by *hiding him* she became liable to the punishment of death for her disobedience to the king's command.

The time soon came, however, when she could conceal him no longer. She ascertained that all her efforts would now prove vain, and that if she did not resort to some extraordinary expedient, the child would be cast into the river. In this most distressing state of mind what could she do? We have no doubt that her first resort was to prayer for the divine direction; and this is the only resort of the afflicted—from this they derive comfort, strength and hope. In her extremity God, indeed, appears to have directed her; and, " hoping against hope," she mournfully commenced the preparation. She first made what the Sacred History calls an ark, probably a little boat, just large enough to bear the weight of the child without sinking. This little boat was made of bulrushes. The bulrush was a kind of reed or cane, called papyrus, which grew upon the banks of the Nile in great abundance, and was exceedingly light, and from the bark of which was formed a material on which to write. From this word our term *paper* is derived. Of this light substance, which would so easily float, the mother made her little boat; and to construct it perfectly water tight, she covered it both within and without with slime and pitch. This slime and pitch is supposed to mean that substance which is now generally known under the name *bitumen*, of which there are several kinds. That which is called naptha swims on water, it being considerably lighter. A little boat made of the bark of the cane and covered with bitumen would not only be water tight, but of very remarkable lightness. Into this light vessel, when she could no longer avoid it, the mother put her darling child. She took every means in her power to insure its safety, and then committed it in faith to God. This is the true spirit of dependance upon God. We must employ the means which He has provided, and then submit all to His wise and sovereign disposal.

After having made this little boat, and put her son within it, this afflicted mother proceeded to the banks of the river Nile to hide the child, where she thought no enemy would think of looking for him. She deposited the boat among the " flags " which grew on the banks of the river. These flags are of the same species with the reeds or rushes of which the boat was built. They grow in immense numbers oh the banks of the Nile, and sometimes rise to the height of 30 or 40 feet. There are two reasons which may have led the mother of the child to place him here. In the first place, as the " flags " or reeds were growing in great numbers, a little ark if placed among them would be less likely to be discovered; and, in the second place, a river always runs less rapidly where it has the kind of obstruction which reeds oppose to its progress. Here, therefore, there was less danger of the ark being carried away. But, after all, these precautions would have amounted to nothing, if God had not seen fit, for the accomplishment of his own wise designs, to take care of this little helpless infant. After this was done, this tender mother was compelled to leave it and return; for had she staid to watch the issue of her plans, it would at once have excited the attention of the cruel officers, and have directed them to the place of its concealment. She went home with a heavy, though certainly not with a desponding heart, for we have reason to believe that she trusted in the Lord, and looked for some manifestation of his mercy in behalf of the child of her faith and prayers. She did not, however, leave her little one in this dangerous predicament without having some one to watch the issue. His little sister Miriam, who is supposed to have been about eight or ten years of age, was placed to observe all that happened. Even she did not dare to go very near, but, as the history tells us, "stood afar off," so that, though she could see where the ark was, she might not be suspected.

It is a wise saying, and a wonderfully true one, that "man's extremity is God's opportunity." What now occurred showed that the whole matter had been ordered and arranged by the hand of God. The ark had lain but a little while floating among the reeds, when directed by the providence of God, the daughter of king Pharaoh, attended by her

maidens, came down from her father's royal palace to bathe in the river. In countries where the weather is always hot, as it is in Egypt, bathing is one of the greatest luxuries that can be enjoyed; and in those early days the great people were more accustomed to bathe in the rivers than they are at present. We do not know from the Bible the name of Pharaoh's daughter, but we are told elsewhere that it was *Thermuthis.* While she was bathing, her maids amused themselves by walking along the banks; but she herself appears first to have seen the little ark among the reeds. No sooner had she seen it than she sent one of her maids to bring it; and when it was brought she opened it. No doubt she was surprised when she found that it contained a little child; and the sacred history tells us that the "babe wept, and that she had compassion on him." This was natural. Who could see a little helpless child thus exposed to danger without the feeling of compassion? surely, no one of the female sex. The stern executioner of her father might, indeed, have torn the child from the protection of the ark, and have cast it off into the middle of the Nile; but the heart of the king's daughter was melted into compassion, and the first remark which she made was, "This is one of the Hebrew's children." She knew what her father had commanded. She knew that it was to evade this order that even a mother was forced to leave her child thus exposed, and God softened her heart, so that she determined that this one at least should not be destroyed. But the child was too young for her to take away: what could she do? Now see the hand of God's over-ruling providence. When Miriam saw the maid of the king's daughter take up the ark and carry it to her mistress, she ran down to the place, and no sooner did she hear the king's daughter say, " This is one of the Hebrew children," than she said, " shall I go and call thee one of the Hebrew women, that she may nurse the child for thee ?" She was told to go ; and she very soon brought the mother of the little boy. Into her hands Pharaoh's daughter committed the precious trust, saying, " Take this child, and nurse it for me, and I will give thee thy wages." And the mother took the child away and nursed it. Thus, by a series of the most wonderful dispensations, this little boy, but a few hours before exposed on the waters, among the reeds of the Nile, in a simple ark of bul-rushes, was rescued from the perils of his situation, and committed, by the daughter of the king, to the arms of his *own mother*. It is likely, though this we offer merely as a conjecture, that the daughter of Pharaoh was so struck with the horrible cruelty of her fa-ther, that she induced him to repeal the com-mand which he had given for the destruction of the Hebrew children. This dreadful de-

cree, we are persuaded, could not have continued long in force, as we read, that when the
Hebrews left Egypt, which was only forty
years after, there was an immense number of
children among them. Let all this be as it
may, one thing is certain—under the protection of the king's daughter, this little boy was
no longer in danger. We are told that he
grew; and although it is not recorded how
old he was, yet probably as soon as he was
weaned, he was taken by his mother to the
palace of the king, and there given into the
hands of his daughter. From that time she
adopted him; and he thus, according to the
custom of the times, became her son, enjoy-
ing all the benefits and privileges which would
have belonged to him if he had actually been
her own child. In order to commemorate the
remarkable occurrence of his preservation, she
called his name MOSES, " because," she said,
" I drew him out of the water;" the Hebrew
word for Moses being derived from a verb
which signifies " to draw out," and which
word is only used in Scripture in reference
to the act of drawing out of water. This is
the first place in the Bible in which the name
of Moses is mentioned. It is not the first
time in which it is mentioned in our history,
for we have frequently called him by that
name that we might be understood. We shall
now always use his name, as we continue his
wonderful and interesting history.

C

CHAPTER V.

*The early Education which Moses received
in the court of Pharaoh.—Moses visits
his brethren.—Kills an Egyptian—is
obliged to fly, and goes to the land of
Midian.*

Moses himself being the writer of the history contained in the book of Exodus, does
not see fit to give any minute account of his own
learning.   He neither tells us the course of
studies which he pursued, nor the progress
which he made.   All the direct information
which we can gather from his own account
is, that he was adopted by the daughter of
Pharaoh, and brought up as her own son.
This included, of course, the best education
which the land of Egypt could afford.   But
though Moses is silent, we have other sources
of information, which are implicitly to be relied on ; and this information is to be found
in the Acts of the Apostles.   It happened on
a certain occasion, that Stephen, one of the
deacons appointed by the apostles just after
the outpouring of the spirit on the day of
Pentecost, was obliged to defend himself before the Jewish council, against a slanderous
charge of blasphemy.   In conducting his de-

fence, which will be found in the 7th chapter of the Acts, he went through the history of the Israelites, commencing with the call of Abraham. When he comes to speak of the history of the children of Israel in Egypt, he tells us that " Moses was learned in all the wisdom of the Egyptians, and mighty in words and deeds."

The learning of the Egyptians principally consisted in what we now call astronomy, mathematics, arithmetic, geometry, mechanics, music, natural history, medicine, chemistry, agriculture, and a little of navigation. They had another portion of learning, which was confined to the priests, and called hieroglyphics, which means a kind of writing by figures instead of words. We cannot employ our time, however, in these inquiries, even though they might be useful, as they would keep us too long from our history.

In every thing which can be connected with the learning of the Egyptians, therefore, we are authorized by Stephen to say, that Moses was instructed, and it was in this way that God filled his mind with knowledge, in order that he might be qualified to act the distinguished part which he had been chosen to perform. For all learning is useless, unless it can be employed in some way towards the promotion of the glory of God, and the good of our fellow-creatures. Many learned men only use their learning to dishonour God, but

terrible will be their destiny. Let us try to
be wise in all profitable learning, but let us
glorify God and do good; and, above all,
never neglect that which is the only true
wisdom—the knowledge and the love of
God.

The sacred history leaves a long interval
between the time when Moses was adopted
by the daughter of Pharaoh, and the period
when he commenced his more active career.
This interval can hardly be less than 35 years,
and during this time he was engaged in bringing his education to perfection. But it is not
to be supposed that his time was principally
occupied in laying up those stores of human
learning for which the Egyptians were so
celebrated. There can he no rational ground
of doubt that he was engaged in making himself fully acquainted with all the particulars
connected with the religion of his fathers. It
would be an interesting task, though not exactly suited to the business of history, to try
to ascertain the principles of religion as held
by the patriarchs, and handed down from
father to son in the traditions of that early
age. This, however interesting it might be,
would lead to a discussion far too lengthened
for a work of this kind; neither would it be
appropriate, inasmuch as the sacred history
does not tell us what, or whether any, ad-
vances were made by Moses in the knowledge
of the Jewish religion. All that we feel the

least authority even to conjecture is, that one intended, as Moses was, for so conspicuous a part in the history of God's chosen people, could not have passed thirty-five years of his life without making investigations into the nature and peculiarities of that true religion which was professed by his parents and his people. He was surrounded by a nation of idolaters. He lived in an idolatrous court, but he himself must have been kept from the sin of idolatry, which God always hates, as it is direct rebellion against him. Be all these things as they may, however, we have no sources of authentic information, and we must take up the history, content to leave about thirty-five years of the life of Moses—a blank as to interesting or valuable incidents.

It came to pass in those days when Moses was grown, and when, according to the testimony of Stephen, he was forty years of age, he went from the court of Pharaoh to visit his brethren. Whether he had ever done this before or not we have no means of information, and consequently conjecture is useless. But on this occasion he observed with sorrow the hard servitude under which his brethren were suffering, and it naturally excited his commiseration. He might have heard of it before, but there is nothing like the sight of human misery to awaken the sympathies of our hearts. We read of the dreadful and cruel superstitions in which the heathen are involved,

c 2

and it produced but a passing emotion of pity, and perhaps contempt; but what a difference would be made in our feelings could we be placed for a little while where we could see these things. Here a woman throwing herself into a fire to be burned with the dead body of her husband; there a mother casting her little child into the river Ganges to be drowned; in another place, hundreds throwing themselves under the huge wheels of an idol's chariot, to be crushed to death. Oh, how happy are our eyes that we are not compelled to see these things; and happy would it be for us if our hearts could adequately feel for the wretched condition of those who are thus sunk in ignorance and spiritual death.

But to return, Moses *saw* the terrible sufferings of his people, and his mind was overwhelmed. He observed in one place an Egyptian beating a Hebrew, with most unmerciful severity, and his indignation was roused. By a sudden impulse he determined to take the part of his oppressed brethren, and having looked all round to see that no person was near, he slew the Egyptian, and buried him in the sand. We should be entirely at a loss to account for this transaction, and should hardly know in what way to speak of it, were we not furnished here also with an explanation by Stephen. From what is said in the Acts, we gather that the expression in Ex-

odus, " when he saw that there was no man,"
only means, that there was no other Egyptian
present or within sight, who could make a report to the king, for that there were many of
the Hebrews present there can be little doubt,
as Stephen tells us, the object which Moses had
in view in this transaction, was to impress on
the minds of his brethren, that he was ready to
undertake to lead them in a revolt against the
Egyptian power.   He did not kill the Egyptian out of any malice: he appears to have
done it while defending his Hebrew brother;
and wished it to be understood as the signal
of a revolution.   This appears to us not a
mere conjecture, but directly authorized by the
language of Scripture; and lest there should
be any misunderstanding, we will quote, word
for word, what Stephen says:—" And when
he (Moses) was full 40 years old, it came
into his heart to visit his brethren, the children
of Israel. And seeing one of them suffer
wrong he defended him, and avenged him that
was oppressed, and smote the Egyptian; *for
he supposed his brethren would have understood how that God by his hand would deliver them; but they understood not.*"   Here
it unquestionably appears, that Moses intended
by this transaction to intimate to them, that
he, under some divine impulse, was ready
to lead them in throwing off the yoke of
Egyptian servitude.   This will give a most
satisfactory account of the whole affair.

It appears, however, that the Israelites were not yet prepared for so decisive a movement. Slavery always oppresses the mind as much as it does the body, and the people required some much more powerful excitement. No person being present to witness what Moses had done, except his brethren the Israelites, who he very naturally supposed would not inform against him, Moses returned to the court of Pharaoh that day without any apprehension. The next day he went again to see how it was with his brethren, and on his way he found two of the Hebrews fighting; a most distressing occurrence when brethren quarrel. Here, as every good man would have done, he determined to act the part of a mediator, and tried to make them friends again. After ascertaining which of the two was most to blame, he accosted him, and said, " wherefore dost thou smite thy fellow ?" It happened to Moses, as it very unfortunately happens to those who would try to reconcile differences among brethren, that he received no thanks for his kindness, but rather insulting and injurious language. Whenever an individual is engaged in a business which he cannot justify, and yet feels too proud to confess himself wrong, and too much irritated to hearken to reason, he generally adds one sin to another. It was the case here. The man who was in the wrong, instead of desisting, and confessing that he was wrong, turned round upon Moses, and said, " Who made thee a prince or a judge over us ?. Wilt thou kill me as thou didst the Egyptian yesterday ?" This was insulting and unkind and ungrateful, but when men are in a passion they care not what they say or do.

Moses now became justly alarmed. He was persuaded that it would be no longer possible to keep the matter a secret, seeing that some of his own brethren were ready to turn against him, and he prepared to meet the consequences. Whether or not he returned to the court of Pharaoh, we are not able to say ; nor how long it was before the report reached the ears of the king. But as soon as Pharaoh heard it, he sought to take the life of Moses, for by the laws of Egypt, the killing of an Egyptian, whether he was bond or free, was punishable by death. This however we are not to consider the real reason, why king Pharaoh was determined to kill Moses. He was afraid that he might put himself at the head of the people of Israel, and thus revolt from his authority and probably overthrow his kingdom. Under circumstances of this kind, it was certainly the dictate of prudence to fly far beyond the reach of the power of Pharaoh, and to do this Moses thought it best to go into the land of Midian. This land of Midian is very different from that which is spoken of in many other parts of Scripture, under the title of the land of the Midianites, which was East of the Dead Sea,

and south of Moab.   The land of Midian to
which Moses fled, was a part of Arabia Petrea,
on the eastern shore of the Dead Sea, and
very near the extreme southern part of the
Peninsula of Arabia, and close by Mount Sinai.   On the map which accompanies this volume you will find a city marked Midian, which
is supposed to be somewhere near the place
where Moses took up his temporary resi-
dence.   It was a country very thinly inhabited,
and which, not being very productive of any
of the luxuries of life, had very little intercourse of any kind with the land of Egypt.
On these accounts, Moses was sure to be un-
known, and even if he had been known, the
king of Egypt had no authority over that
country.   Indeed there was no well established
government there of any kind, but the inhabitants were principally like the wandering
tribes of Arabs, who live there at the present
day.   But besides this, the mind of Moses
was no doubt directed to this place by the special influence of God, who had great purposes
to effect, and required a good deal of preparatory discipline on the part of Moses,
thoroughly to fit him for his work.

CHAPTER VI.

History of Moses in the land of Midian.—
He assists the daughters of Jethro, and
marries in that land.

WHEN Moses thought he had fled far enough
to be beyond the reach of Pharaoh, he began
to think more seriously of his forlorn and destitute situation. He was in a strange country,
without friends and without protection ; and
besides this, he was without any kind of knowledge as to the means of providing himself
with a home, and means of support. In this
condition he chose one of the wisest expe-
dients which could possibly be thought of, in
a country like the one in which he wandered.
"He sat down by a well," the history tells
us : Now some of our young readers may ask
where was the wisdom of this—might he not
better have followed any path he could find, till
it led him to some settlement ? No : we will
show how he acted wisely.

In those eastern countries, and especially in
Arabia, where water is very scarce, there are
large public wells dug, where some spring or
fountain may have been discovered, and these
wells are resorted to by the inhabitants for
many miles around for the purpose of watering

their flocks and herds. In the course of his wearisome journey, Moses came, or rather the Lord directed him to one of these wells; and he thought, now I will wait here till somebody comes; for then, at all events, I shall obtain information: and so putting his trust in God, he at once sat down by the well, knowing that it could not be long before some one would be there. Thus it is that God leads his people, and makes all things work together for their good. The little circumstance of Moses sitting down by this well, was connected with some of the most important concerns of his eventful life; so true it is, that in the hand of God the smallest events are connected with the most stupendous purposes.

In the providence of God, matters turned out just as Moses expected; for in a very short time, he saw a large flock of sheep coming to the well, under the care of seven young women, whom he afterwards found to be the daughters of Jethro, the Priest, or Prince of Midian, for the Hebrew word sometimes means either. Who or what this Jethro was, is not easy for us to determine. All we know with certainty is, that he was a descendant of Abraham; for *Midian*, from whom this part of the country took its name, was a son of Abraham; by his second wife Keturah, whom he married after the death of Sarah. This is told us in the 2d verse of the 25th chapter of Genesis. At the city called Midian there is a well which, even down to this day, the Mahometans say, is the well at which Moses saw the daughters of Jethro. All this, however, is doubtful. Nothing is said in Scripture to enable us to identify the place.

We have said that while Moses was sitting at this well, the daughters of Jethro came with the flocks of their father; and it seems quite strange to us, in these days, to hear of the daughters of a prince engaged in such an occupation. But we must remember that so far back as 3350 years ago, when this transaction occurred, the habits of people were very different from what they now are. Then even the daughters of the greatest persons did not think it beneath their dignity to be engaged in domestic occupations. To this very day, the daughters of some of the greatest Arabian chiefs attend the flocks of their fathers; and the heathen poet, Homer, tells us, that the seven children of the king of Thebes, one of the chief cities of ancient Greece, did the same thing, and so did Antiphus, the son of Priam, king of Troy; and so did Anchises, the father of Virgil's hero, Æneas. So that we well know the custom of those times, and need not be surprised at the transaction which is here related.

While the daughters of Jethro were preparing to have their flocks watered, a circumstance occurred, which gave Moses an excellent opportunity both of doing a kind action,

D

and of getting particularly acquainted. Some of the neighbouring shepherds came to water their flocks at the same well, and as they did not choose to remain till the flocks of Jethro were watered, they drove them away, and were about to help themselves, and thus make the others wait. This, as might naturally be expected, excited the displeasure of Moses, and he very properly interfered to prevent the helpless females from being imposed upon in this way. The shepherds appear to have been intimidated by Moses, or perhaps they became ashamed of their uncivil treatment, and stood off for awhile. But Moses was not satisfied with merely taking the part of these young women; he added his own assistance in their work; he helped them, and watered their flock; and by this means they were able to get their flocks home much earlier than usual. This attracted the particular attention of their father; and he asked them how they came to get home so early. They told him the case, just as it occurred, except that they made a mistake about the character of Moses. They supposed he was an Egyptian, as he probably had an Egyptian dress on.

When Jethro heard the account, he appears to be surprised that they had been so thoughtless as not to invite him to their father's house; for in those days, when there were no places of public entertainment, such as our stagehouses and hotels, &c., strangers were

always welcome to the hospitality of any family where they might feel disposed to stop.
It would be an act of great imprudence for
young ladies to invite to their homes every
stranger who might render them any occasional attention or assistance, because by
this means many improper persons might get
into a family. The state of society is very
different now from what it was then. At
that time when manners were more pure and
simple, and when hospitality was more abso-
lutely necessary, there would have been no
impropriety in their inviting Moses to their
father's house. But, very strangely, they
had forgotten it; and Jethro certainly seems
to have given them a gentle rebuke for their
want of gratitude and consideration. He
says, " Where is he? Why is it that ye
have left the man?" And then, without waiting for any of their excuses, he added, " Call
him, that he may eat bread."

Moses, as might reasonably be expected,
appears very gladly to have accepted the invitation; and being a stranger and destitute,
and having no definite object in view, except
to keep out of the way of Pharaoh, he made
up his mind to accept the offer of Jethro, to
remain with him, probably with an intention
of rendering him assistance in his various em-
ployments.

How long Moses lived with Jethro it is
not easy to say with any great precision.

The probability is, however, that it was somewhere about 40 years, for he does not appear to have returned to Egypt, until he was 80 years of age. In the meantime the prince of Midian being satisfied with Moses, and conceiving a great friendship for him, gave him one of his daughters as a wife, and thus brought him into his own family by the most sacred and endearing ties. How long Moses had been with Jethro before he was married is a question which Scripture leaves undecided, and which, of course, is a matter of no kind of consequence to us. Suffice it to say, that the daughter of Jethro whom he married, was Zipporah, and eventually they had two children; one of them Moses called *Gershom*, which means a desolate stranger, and the other he called *Eliezer*, which means, God my help.

As Jethro was a descendant of Abraham, the probability is, that he was in possession of the true religion, and in the slight history which is given of his family, there is nothing to shake this opinion. If they were truly pious, as well as possessing a knowledge of true religion, then must the days of Moses have passed quickly and happily along. In those early ages there was nothing more calculated to excite and keep alive pious sensibilities than the pastoral life: having few alterations of condition, and constant though not laborious occupation, time glided onward in a smooth and even current, with few temptations, and few strong enticements to great transgressions. How often is our blessed Lord in the Scriptures addressed under the characteristic and tender appellation of a shepherd. "Tell me, O thou whom my soul loveth, where thou feedest, where thou makest thy flock to rest at noon. For why should I be as one that turneth aside by the flocks of thy companions?" Our Lord calls himself the Good Shepherd; and He is not only so because he leads his people into green pastures and beside the still waters, but because he even laid down his life for the sheep that they might be rescued out of the hand of the destroyer.

CHAPTER VII.

Moses in the land of Midian.—God calls to him out of the burning bush.—Orders him to return to Egypt.—His reluctance.—God's condescension.—Final acquiescence of Moses.

WHILE Moses remained in the land of Midian, in the quiet pursuits of the pastoral life, and no doubt improving the leisure which he enjoyed to his advancement in personal piety, the people of Israel were still suffering under

D 2

the rigour of their cruel master. The king, under whose reign Moses was born, and from whose wrath he fled, died during the period in which he sojourned in Midian. But this king was succeeded by another, who, from the incidental intimations of the sacred history, we should suppose was equally if not more cruel than the last; for it is told us, that now " the children of Israel sighed by reason of their bondage." Its severity and its long duration had discouraged and disheartened them, but it produced one effect, which, in the ways of God, seems to be most generally connected with a change of circumstances for the better. Their heavy affliction led them to apply to God for relief; and when afflictions of any kind serve to cut up by the root all earthly dependencies, and constrain the soul to flee to God, and to him alone, then they appear to answer the purpose for which they were intended, and brighter days may reasonably be expected. The people cried unto the Lord, and God heard their cry: he bore in remembrance the promise which he had made to Abraham, to Isaac, and to Jacob; for he never forgets his word. The time appointed to fulfil this promise had now arrived; and we will now point out the method in which God saw fit that Moses should be connected with it.

At the time in which the bondage of the children of Israel had reached its height

Moses had been a resident in Midian, it is supposed, about 40 years. His principal occupation had no doubt been to tend the flocks while they were out at pasture. On one of these occasions he had driven the flocks, for the advantage of better pasturage, as far as the mountain which is called Horeb, spoken of as the Mount of God; probably because God afterwards gave the Law from a part of the same range which had the name of Sinai. While he was employed in watching the sheep, as they fed on the green grass, or as they gamboled on the gentle slopes of the mountains; and while he, no doubt, occupied his mind in meditation on the ways and the works of God, his attention was directed to a circumstance most singularly mysterious. All at once a bush, which was a little on one side of the place where he was sitting, appeared on fire—it actually burned; but, as it burned, not one leaf was withered, and not one little twig was destroyed. For the moment he does not appear to have understood it as any thing intended to attract his attention to any special revelation. It struck him with very great surprise; and he says, " I will now turn aside, and see this great sight, why the bush is not burnt." While he was engaged in the contemplation of this mysterious sight, and was advancing nearer and nearer for the purpose of investigating this singular phenomenon, he was arrested by a voice from the

midst of the bush, which called him by his name, and directed him to take off the shoes, or rather sandals, which were on his feet, because the place was hallowed or holy by the presence of God. Moses must have been astonished at the vision and the voice; how much more so when he discovered who it was that spoke to him. The person speaking to Moses on this solemn occasion is called, in the second verse of the third chapter of Exodus, the " Angel of the Lord;" and yet this very same one called the Angel, could not have been any created being, for in the sixth verse of the same chapter, he tells Moses who he is, "*I* am the God of thy father, the God of Abraham, the God of Isaac, and the God of

Jacob:" and then the history tells us, that Moses "hid his face, for he was afraid to look upon GOD." And in the 14th verse of the same chapter, where Moses asks God what he shall tell the people, God answers him in these striking terms, " I AM THAT I AM, and he said, Thus shalt thou say unto the children of Israel, I AM hath sent me unto you." In these things our readers are requested to observe one most remarkable particular, which is, that the Angel takes the name of *God*, and consequently he could not have been one of those beings whom we call Angels, and who are described by the apostle Paul, as " ministering spirits sent forth to minister for them who shall be heirs of salvation." This Angel who appeared to Moses must have been infinitely higher than any created Angel, and could not have been any other than that blessed Being who afterwards took our nature upon him, and appeared on earth in the person of the Lord Jesus Christ. Our Lord Jesus Christ is, by the prophet Malachi, called the Messenger, or Angel of the Covenant. This was the same person who afterwards appeared on Mount Sinai, and delivered the Law to Moses. This is the same person who, on various occasions, had appeared to the ancient patriarchs in a visible form, prophetic of his future incarnation. Respecting God the father, it is said in John, i. 18. " No man hath seen God at any time." And

again, in ch. v. 37, " Ye have neither heard
his' voice at any time, nor seen his shape."
The Angel, then, who here appeared to Moses, who afterwards conducted the children of
Israel through the wilderness ; who gave the
Law from Mount Sinai, and who was the
king of Israel, was no other than him who
" being in the form of God, took upon him
the form of a servant." It is also worthy
of remark, that the same Angel says, when
asked his name, " I AM THAT I AM," and this
is the very term which our Saviour uses of
himself in his conversations with the Jews,
as recorded in John, viii. 58. " Before Abraham was I AM."

After this solemn announcement of himself
as God, the Lord proceeds to tell Moses the
reasons why he had made himself known to
him. He stated that he had seen with tenderness and compassion the wretched situation
to which the Israelites were reduced by reason
of the severity of the bondage under which
they suffered, and he calls them " my people ;" for, notwithstanding their ignorance,
their degradation, and their wickedness, they
were the children of Abraham, of Isaac, and
of Jacob, to whom he had promised his blessing, and he was determined to do them good
for the sake of their fathers. Yet He did not
bring this good upon them till he saw they
were humbled under their sufferings, and cried
unto him for help. It is thus that God deals

with sinners. He will do them good for Jesus' sake, who died upon the cross as an atonement for sin; but never will he receive them to his love until they repent of their sins, and lay hold of the hope of the gospel. But to return to Moses. God declared to him, that the time was come when He intended to deliver the Israelites out of Egypt, and bring them into the lovely land of Canaan—the land then possessed by people called the Canaanites, the Hittites, the Amorites, the Perizzites, the Hivites, and the Jebusites; and he tells Moses that He was the person who was to act as his agent and minister in this great and glorious enterprise. Moses at once declined the appointment, as if he doubted his qualifications: " Who am I that I should go?" Remark here the great contrast which 40 years' experience had made in the mind of Moses. He had once thought that he was qualified for this work, and he set about it, with considerable zeal, by killing an Egyptian, but now when he was incomparably better qualified, he became more alive to his insufficiency. " This was in a great measure the effect of increasing knowledge of God and of himself, but there was also a deep sense of the vast difficulty of the business, not without some culpable fear of Pharaoh and the Egyptians, and of contempt and opposition from Israel. Before, self-confidence mingled with and assumed the appearance of

strong faith and great zeal; but now some
degree of sinful distrust of God was associated with deep humility, and induced him
timidly to shift, as well as humbly to decline,
the important service. So very defective are
the strongest graces, and the best duties even
of the most eminent saints." In relation to
any service to be rendered to the cause of
God, any man may reasonably ask, " Who
is sufficient for these things?" but the answer of the gospel is ready :—" My grace is
sufficient for thee." So it was in the case of
Moses. No sooner had he said, " Who am
I, that I should go unto Pharaoh, and that *I*
should bring the children of Israel out of
Egypt?" than God is ready with the encouraging answer, " Certainly *I* will be with
thee." As if He had said, I am not going to
send you on so difficult a business, and then
leave you to yourself. No: I know all the
obstacles. I know without me you can do
nothing. What I send you to do, *I* will enable you to do: fear not. It was a similar
promise of their blessed Master which gave
the Apostles their holy and heavenly confidence. Matt. xxviii. 18—20. "And Jesus
came and spake unto them, saying, All power
is given unto me in heaven and in earth. Go
ye, therefore, and teach all nations, baptizing
them in the name of the Father, and of the
Son, and of the Holy Ghost: teaching them
to observe all things whatsoever I have com-

manded you : and, lo, I am with you always, even unto the end of the world. Amen."

After God had thus graciously encouraged Moses, he gave him a sign or token, by telling him, that when all these things happened, he should serve God or worship him on that very mountain. This was a test of the faith of Moses. God says, when you have succeeded in bringing Israel out of Egypt through my power, you shall know that I have given you the commission, by coming to this very place where we now are. Moses believed God, and was encouraged. Still, while he was in Egypt, he had seen and known so much of the ingratitude of the Israelites, that he expressed his fears to God that they would not receive him—that they might probably ask him again, who had made him a ruler or judge over them; and he therefore humbly asks of God to permit him to know what he should say to them; and that if they asked him who sent him, he might have some answer to give. God here, also, most graciously condescends to give him the most full and satisfactory information. " And God said unto Moses, I AM THAT I AM: and he said, Thus shalt thou say unto the children of Israel, I AM hath sent me unto you." Ex. iii. 14. And lest that should not be sufficient, he furnishes him with an answer which the people could more distinctly understand. "And God said moreover unto Moses, Thus

E

shalt thou say unto the children of Israel, **The Lord** God of your fathers, the God of Abraham, the God of Isaac, and the God of Jacob, hath sent me unto you: this *is* my name for ever, and this *is* my memorial unto all generations." ver. 15. God then tells him to enter into an explanation of what had now occurred, and to place before them the promises previously made:—" Go, and gather the elders of Israel together, and say unto them, The Lord God of your fathers, the God of Abraham, of Isaac, and of Jacob, appeared unto me, saying, I have surely visited you, and *seen* that which is done to you in Egypt: And I have said, I will bring you up out of the affliction of Egypt unto the land of the Canaanites, and the Hittites, and the Amorites, and the Perizzites, and the Hivites, and the Jebusites, unto a land flowing with milk and honey." ver. 16, 17.

We cannot pass on to other particulars of this interesting history, without asking the very solemn attention of our readers to a few remarks of the pious Bishop Beveridge on the expression " I am. To the mind of a Christian the extract will convey the most lively feelings of gratification, and it may touch the hearts of others." " When God speaks of himself," says our Author, " and his own eternal Essence, he saith, *I am that I am*, so when he speaks of himself in reference to his creatures, and especially his people, he says *I am*. He doth not say, *I am their friend, their father, their protector*. He doth not say, *I am their light, their life, their guide, their strength, their tower;* but only *I am*. He sets as it were his hand to a blank, that his people may write under it what they please that is good for them. As if he should say, *Are they weak? I am strength. Are they poor? I am riches. Are they in trouble? I am comfort. Are they sick? I am health. Are they dying? I am life. Have they nothing? I am all things. I am wisdom and power, I am justice and mercy, I am grace and goodness; I am glory, beauty, holiness, eminency, supereminency, perfection, all-sufficiency, eternity*. Jehovah I am. *Whatsoever is amiable in itself, or desirable unto them*, that I am. *Whatsoever is pure and holy, whatsoever is great or pleasant, whatsoever is good or needful to make men happy*, that I am. So that, in short, God here represents himself unto us as an universal good, and leaves us to make the application of it to ourselves, according to our several wants, capacities, and desires, by saying only in general, I AM."

But now to return to the history. God graciously condescended to assure Moses, that his countrymen would listen to his voice, and ordered him, in company with the elders of Israel—the more aged and distinguished men among their tribes, to go and present himself before the king of Egypt, and to de-

mand, in the name of his God, permission to
go three days' journey into the wilderness, in
order that they might, without any hindrance
or molestation, make a solemn sacrifice to the
God of their fathers. At the same time,
however, God who reads the hearts of men,
and knows what their determinations will be,
informed Moses that Pharaoh would not by
any means grant their request. It may at
once, then, be asked, if God knew what
Pharaoh would do, why did he send Moses
on a fruitless errand. Every difficulty of this
kind arises out of a defective view of God's
moral government. Does a master lose
his right to give a command, because he may
be persuaded that his servant will refuse
to obey? Does a father forfeit his right to
obedience, because a child may choose to
be rebellious? If I knew perfectly well from
the perverse and stubborn nature of a child
that he would not obey my commands,
ought I to withhold a command which was
connected with his welfare? Certainly not.
The honour of God was concerned that,
whether Pharaoh would or would not obey,
he should give the command, and thus
show his right to be obeyed, and take away
all shadow of excuse which might otherwise
be made. Besides this, God purposed to visit
the land of Egypt, for the abominations of
the people, and for their iniquitous treatment
of the Israelites; and in order to show that

his punishment would be just, he saw fit to make a direct demand upon the king. Lest Moses should be discouraged by being told that the king would not let the people go when he was so solemnly required, God further informed him, that after he had punished the Egyptians according as he saw fit, then the king would eventually comply with the demand. He informed him further, that he would make the Egyptians so desirous of the departure of the Israelites, that they would be willing to do any thing, and give any thing to hasten that departure. We shall soon see that all this took place as was predicted; but before we come to the tremendous scenes which occurred as preparatory to that result, there is a circumstance which requires some explanation.

We are told, that God ordered every woman to *borrow* of her neighbour jewels of silver, and jewels of gold, and also clothing, and thus to spoil the Egyptians. Infidel writers have improperly made a great handle of this circumstance, and have said, that here is a direct command to be thieves. As we use the word " to borrow" in our language, it means to ask the loan of something which we intend to return, and if we do not return it, it is just as bad as stealing. But it ought to be remembered, that the Bible was written in Hebrew, and that the Hebrew word which is translated

borrow, only signifies *to ask.* All that the
Israelites, therefore, did, was to *ask* or demand of the Egyptians such things as they
needed or might need in their journey; and
what they received was justly due them as an
equivalent for the long and painful services
which they had rendered.

There is one thing very remarkable in this
history of Moses, as written by himself. He
does not pretend to hide or excuse his own
follies, and his wicked opposition to the declared wishes of God. We see another instance of his perverseness immediately after
God had given him these directions, and notwithstanding that he had been distinctly told
that the people would hearken unto his voice,
he persists in doubting it, and had the teme-
rity to answer God, and say, " But, behold,
they *will not believe me,* nor hearken unto
my voice, for they will say, the Lord hath
not appeared unto thee." This, somewhat
like the incredulity of Thomas, recorded
John xx. 25, appears to have been permitted,
that such abundant evidences might be given
as could leave no room for any reasonable
doubt on the part of the people. Moses at
that time had a rod or staff in his hand: it
was most probable a shepherd's crook. God
saw fit to work a miracle, to show him that
he would be received as the leader of the
people. He told him to throw down the
stick which he held, and no sooner did he

do it, than it was instantly, by the power of God, turned into a serpent, and Moses alarmed at the sight sought to run away. But God called him back, and ordered him, instead of being afraid, to take it by the tail. No sooner did he obey, than the serpent became what it was before, a rod in his hand. But this was not the only miracle by which God condescended to assure him that he should be successful. He told him to put his hand into his bosom, and on taking it out it was covered with leprosy, and became white as snow; and this while the rest of his body was perfectly sound. God again told him to put his hand into his bosom, and when he took it out it was perfectly well as it was at the first. God then told him that if the people would not be convinced by his performing the first miracle, that of turning the rod into a serpent, they would be convinced by the other; and that if the least scruple existed among them after these two miracles had been done before their eyes, he was to take water out of the river, and to pour it on the earth, when it would be turned into blood. All this was done, as we shall hereafter see.

But still Moses had another excuse. When every thing else failed, he told the Lord that he was not *eloquent*, he was not a good speaker, that he was slow of speech, probably he had some hesitation in his speech, something akin to stammering. The gracious God, instead of casting him off as utterly worthless, chose to put to him these interesting questions :—" And the Lord said unto him, Who hath made man's mouth? or who maketh the dumb, or deaf, or the seeing, or the blind? have not I the Lord?" ch. iv. 11 : and then tells him positively—" Now therefore go, and I will be with thy mouth, and teach thee what thou shalt say." ver. 12.

God having thus answered all the objections which Moses had made, and cut short all his excuses, it would be thought that no further difficulty could have been made. But all the objections of Moses, and all his excuses, had been, just as the objections and excuses of sinners now are when urged to repentance, only intended to hide the real unwillingness of his heart; and so, when he found that they would not answer, he came out with the real state of his mind, and intimated to the Lord, that he did not want to go. He probably felt himself so comfortable where he was, and he had lived peaceably so long, that he did not like the danger of the task, and now he declines the honour. It is a wonder that he was not struck dead for his presumption; but God had great designs to answer, and though he declares that his anger was kindled against him for his unbelief and unwillingness, he did not see fit to dismiss him. He took this last excuse away, by telling him that his elder brother, Aaron, who was a good speaker, and had no defect of utterance, should go with him ; that Aaron should speak to the people, and that he should give the necessary instructions. God then told him to take the rod, and go ; and Moses made no more excuses. He saw his error: he repented. He was faithful and zealous, and God was thenceforth his guide and his counsellor, and the power of his hand.

CHAPTER VIII.

Moses departs from Midian.—Takes his family into Egypt.—Is instructed as to his special message to Pharaoh.—Goes to Pharaoh, who refuses to obey God's message. —Considerations connected with the hardening of Pharaoh's heart.

WE have seen in the preceding chapter the condescension of God in removing the difficulties out of the way of Moses, and in enabling him to come to a clear determination to be submissive to the will of his heavenly Father. No sooner had he come to this determination than he carried it into effect. He went immediately to his father-in-law, and stated the case to him, requesting his permission to leave the place where he had so happily passed his days, and go to do the will of the Lord. Jethro made no objections; and God, further to encourage Moses, informed him that those persons who had sought his life while in Egypt were now dead. Moses on his return took his family with him—his wife and his two sons, Gershom and Eliezer. How long he was in accomplishing the journey we do not know; but it must have been two or three days, as they travelled very slow in those times, when journeys were principally performed on foot. All the while, however, God was mindful of Moses, and sent his brother Aaron out into the wilderness to meet him. Their separation had been long, and their meeting was affectionate. According to the custom of those times they kissed each other. As they then went along together towards Egypt, Moses told Aaron all that had occurred; and when they reached the territory of Goshen, they assembled the elders of the children of Israel, told them publicly all that the Lord had directed, and performed the miracles which had been appointed. According to the word of. God, which never fails, the people believed that Moses had been sent to them with a special commission; and they were so encouraged and animated by the prospect of deliverance, that they returned their thanks to God in a solemn act of worship.

We now come to a period in the history of Moses, which is particularly remarkable for its connexion with the punishments which God inflicted on the Egyptians. In a very short time after Moses had satisfied the people of Israel, that he was sent from God to effect their deliverance, he prepared to carry his message to the proud and cruel king of Egypt. He took his brother Aaron with him, and went to the king's palace; and, as soon as they were admitted into the royal presence, they delivered their message in the following plain and simple language :—" Thus saith the Lord, Let my people go, that they may hold a feast unto me in the wilderness." This was a very modest and moderate demand, even if it had not been authorized by God himself; for as the people had been serving the king of Egypt for no less than 80 years at least, in the most abject servitude, it was but little to ask a few days for the service of their God. But as they wished to hold a feast, why did they not ask permission to do it in Egypt? The reason is very clear : their feast must be accompanied with sacrifices to God, and as these sacrifices were of such animals as the Egyptians worshipped, it would not have been judicious nor safe to hold their feast in Egypt, lest the people should have been provoked to injure them.

This demand, however reasonable as it was in itself, and still more important because

it was authorized by the great God, seemed
to produce no effect on the mind of Pharaoh,
except to make him angry. He had done
wrong in reducing the people to slavery, and
he then determines to do more wrong in order
to justify his former conduct, just as most
persons when they commit one sin will prefer
committing several others to keep themselves
in countenance, rather than at once confess
their fault and repent. Pharaoh insolently
and presumptuously replied, " Who is Jehovah ; I know him not, neither will I let Israel
go." Instead of denouncing the vengeance
of God against this unjust king, Moses and
Aaron plead with him for his permission.
They told him, that the Lord, their God, required of them that they should go, and that
if they did not, they should but excite his
anger. They therefore begged of Pharaoh
that he would let them go. Instead of yield-
ing, however, the king grew more and more
angry, and said, " Wherefore do ye, Moses
and Aaron, *let* (that is, hinder) the people
from doing their work. Get you to your
burdens." The anger of Pharaoh led him
into greater acts of injustice. The very day
when he treated the message of God by Moses
so disrespectfully and proudly, he ordered the
burdens of the people to be increased. They
were commanded to make bricks without the
usual supply of straw. The straw was needed
in the manufacture of the bricks, to chop in

fine pieces to mix with clay, or for some other purpose, and had been delivered to them as it was needed; but now the supply was withheld, and they were required to get it as they could. They found it impossible, of course, to do as much work as usual, because they had to go into the fields and gather stubble instead of straw, and then the officers of the children of Israel, whom Pharaoh's task-masters had set over them, were beaten because the same quantity of work was not done. And when they appealed to the king, they were turned away without any redress, but with the insulting language, " Ye are idle ; ye are idle, therefore ye say, let us go and sacrifice to the Lord."

This was a very trying time to Moses, for besides the ill-treatment which he had received from Pharaoh, he was compelled to suffer the reproaches of his own countrymen, just as if he had been the cause of the great hardships which they endured. It so happened, that as the officers who had been appointed to make their complaint to Pharaoh, were returning from their unsuccessful errand, they met Moses and Aaron, and began at once to upbraid them :—" The Lord look upon you and judge you ; because you have made us to be abhorred in the eyes of Pharaoh, and in the eyes of his servants, to put a sword in their hand to slay us." This hurt the feelings and discouraged the spirit of Moses far more

F

than all the cruelty of Pharaoh; for to be re-
proached by those whom we love, and are
trying to serve, is hard to bear.   Under these
circumstances Moses laid the case before the
Lord, but not in such a spirit of faith ·as he
ought to have done, for he seems rather disposed to sink into despondency, and to complain that the Lord had not been kind and
compassionate; so very difficult is it for even
good men always to bear their disappointments
with humility and faith.

All these things, however, were working
out the purposes of God for the good of his
people.   Moses was again assured by God
that every thing should be done which he had
promised, and sent again to tell the people
that his promise should not fail.   Moses went
to the people with this encouraging message
of God, but their spirits were so broken down
by the cruelty with which they had been
treated, that they could hardly be induced to
listen to what he had to say.   How strange
it is, that any one should not be willing to believe what God says ; and the very time when
we ought most to rely on the promises of·
God, is when affliction comes upon us, for
what can enable us to bear it, but a trust in
God ?

This part of the history of Moses, as indeed
almost every other, illustrates the wonderful
long-suffering and patience of God.   Moses
was again discouraged by the fact, that the

Israelites seemed to have lost all hope, and he instead of cheerfully obeying God, begins again to excuse himself, and when God tells him to go to Pharaoh again, he says, My own people will not listen to me, and how am I to expect Pharaoh to listen? And, besides, I have no ability to plead the cause properly; I am not a good speaker. Now all this was mere excuse; but God even then did not forsake his people. He told Moses again that Aaron should be the speaker, and after this Moses never seems to have made any further opposition to the will of God. The sacred History tells us, that at this period Moses was eighty years of age, and Aaron three years older.

But by far the most remarkable thing in the history of Moses at this time, and one which has caused many persons a great deal of perplexity is, that when God ordered Moses to go with the message to Pharaoh, he told him once and again that He would harden Pharaoh's heart, and he would not let the people go. It may be, and has often been asked, if God hardened the heart of Pharaoh how could he help doing what he did? All the difficulty lies in the meaning which we are apt to give to the word *harden*, as if it could be supposed that God could put evil desires and determinations into the heart of any one. We must get rid of this notion first, and then there will be no difficulty. All our readers have no doubt read what God says by the apostle James :—

" God cannot be tempted with evil ;" that is, God can never be tempted to do any thing wrong, for He is infinitely pure and holy ; but the apostle says, " Neither tempteth He any man ;" that is, he never puts wicked thoughts into the hearts of any. But then what does this *hardening* of the heart mean ? The difficulty can now be explained in two ways. 1st Solomon tells us, that because sentence against an evil work is not executed speedily, therefore the heart of the sons of men is *fully set* in them to do evil. Eccles. viii. 11. This was the case with Pharaoh ; for we are told that " when he saw there was respite, he hardened his heart as the Lord had said." Exod. viii. 15. This means, that the goodness of God, in not executing judgment upon him at once for his rebellion, instead of softening his heart, and leading him to repentance as it ought to have done, produced in him a contrary effect, *because* he was *fully set* in his own mind to do evil, and became more and more determined so to do, when he saw that he could, as he supposed, escape. We see this every day ; for who does not observe persons under the afflictions of God's hand, becoming more and more wicked instead of better, and we know that fire, which softens some substances, hardens others. Thus Pharoah, in fact, hardened his own heart.

But there is another way in which God is said to harden the hearts of those who abuse his mercies. He withdraws his spirit from them as a punishment of their sins, and then they are sure to grow worse and worse; for nothing can keep any one from the most dreadful sins but the restraining grace of God. When God then becomes so much displeased. as to determine to leave sinners to do as they wish, then he is said to harden their hearts. Now, as we do not intend to allude to this subject again, we will take the occasion to give some friendly advice to our readers, founded on this dreadful thing which happened to wicked Pharaoh.

The case of Pharaoh, left by the spirit of God to work out his own ruin, ought to teach us all to beware how we harden our hearts against convictions of sin. No persons ever resisted the gracious pleadings of the spirit of God and eventually escaped. We have the instances of the inhabitants of Sodom and Gomorrah. We have the case of Pharaoh, and the case of Felix. It is written, "My spirit shall not always strive with man;" and if the spirit ceases to strive, then the heart of that person is surely hardened. Let this history teach us the importance of immediately accepting the kind offers of God through his son, Jesus Christ. We remember a very interesting anecdote of the ancient Romans :—
A Roman embassador once demanded of king Antiochus to withdraw his armies from the siege of a city which was in friendship with

the Romans. " What time," said the king, " do you allow me to consider whether I shall accept or refuse your demands?" " Your resolution must be taken before you stir beyond the limits of this circle," said the Roman, at the same time drawing a circle round the king. " Before you step over this, you must declare whether you will be the friend or the enemy of Rome." Such a circle God draws round every one. This hour, this very hour, are you called upon to give you hearts to God. You do not know but that at this moment he may be making the last offer of his love. You do not know but if you now reject it, your heart may be hardened, and then nothing but ruin can come. " Behold, now is the accepted time and the day of salvation."

CHAPTER IX.

Moses, by the command of God, works miracles, and brings upon Egypt dreadful plagues.

THERE cannot be one among the readers of this history, we think, who is not acquainted with what the Scripture tells us about the interviews which Moses and Aaron had with

Pharaoh, after the transactions which are
mentioned in the last chapter. According to
the last command of God on the subject,
Moses no more hesitated to go to the king,
and tell him what the Lord would do if he
persisted in refusing to let the people go; and
in order to convince him that he was sent of
God, when Pharaoh said, Show a miracle,
that I may know something about your pretensions, Aaron threw down his rod on the
ground, and in a moment it became a serpent.
Surprising as this was, however, Pharaoh
supposed it was only some trick, similar to
what some of his own magicians or wise men
could play, and so he sent for them, and when
they came they cast their rods on the ground
and they also became serpents. This still
more convinced Pharaoh that Moses and Aaron
were little better than expert jugglers, for his
darkened mind did not understand that for the
purpose of showing the greatness of his own
power, God for a little while permitted the
Egyptian magicians to imitate the miracles of
Moses. Moses, himself, must at the moment
have been very much surprised to see it; but
by this time he had learned to put implicit
faith in God, and to know that it was all intended for some wise purpose. He did not
long remain in this state of perplexity, for the
serpents which the Egyptian magicians produced were immediately swallowed up by the
serpent formed by the power of God from the

rod of Moses. Several miracles were performed by the Egyptian magicians; but they
were all intended the more signally to confirm the power of the true God, and establish
the divine commission of Moses. After two
attempts in which the magicians were permitted to succeed, they made a third, but
God saw fit to stop them, and then they confessed that it was the power of God. Still
Pharaoh was deaf to the entreaties of Moses,
and, like all hardened sinners, he seemed bent
on his own destruction.

In the whole history of the world, there is
scarcely a more awful account than that of
the ten plagues which God sent on the land
of Egypt. And yet how many persons read
the history without noticing the real and peculiar meaning of those plagues. We have
no doubt that we shall convey some new and
interesting ideas to the minds of our young
readers at least, while we very briefly go on
to show what God meant by the peculiar form
in which these plagues were sent.

Of all the nations on the face of the earth,
the Egyptians, for a people who were really
wise in a great many things, were the most
stupid and senseless idolaters. There was
scarcely any thing that flew in the air, or crawl-
ed on the earth, or swam in the river, which
was not in some way worshipped by them.
And thus, they neither believed nor worshipped
the true God; and they despised and hated

the Israelites because they did worship the one living and true God. This great God, who has declared that he is a jealous God, and will not give his glory to another, was determined to show that he alone was God, and that there was none else, and consequently all the *plagues* which were sent upon Egypt as a punishment for their treatment of the people of Israel, were made to show that the *gods of Egypt* were of no account. Every one of the plagues, except the last, was directed against the Egyptians through the medium of their objects of idolatry, and this renders a consideration of those *plagues* more important and interesting than it otherwise would be. And this is the reason why we intend to spend a little time in examining the subject.

The *first plague* was the turning of the waters of the *Nile* into *blood*. This celebrated river was considered one of the very greatest of the *Egyptian deities*, and all the fish which were in it were worshipped as subordinate or inferior gods. When their river then was turned into blood, and their fish died, it showed that these their gods were subject to the power of the great Jehovah.

The *second plague* was that of *frogs*, an animal to the Egyptians peculiarly loathsome; and this was another evidence of the weakness of their god, the *Nile*, for it could not avoid sending forth these loathsome creatures.

The *third plague* was that of *lice*, which came upon every man and beast throughout the whole land. This was also a plague aimed at the idolatry of Egypt, for no one could go near their altars on whom such an insect as this was found. The priests, in order to avoid impurities of this kind, shaved their heads and beards every day, and wore only light linen garments. This, therefore, was a very severe judgment upon the idolatry of Egypt, as no act of their worship could be performed while it lasted. The magicians, themselves, appear to have been particularly struck with this miracle, and confessed that it was " the finger of God."

The *fourth plague* was that of *flies*. The fly was one of the gods of Egypt, and is here made the instrument in the hand of the true God of punishing his own senseless worshippers.

The *fifth plague* was the *murrain* among cattle. This was a kind of disease which carried them off in great numbers ; and this plague struck at the very root of their idolatry, which was the worship of beasts. Under the names of *Osiris, Isis, Ammon,* and *Pan,* they worshipped the *bull,* and the *ram,* and the *he goat,* and the *heifer*; but yet the true God, at the word of Moses, sent a disease which killed these animals as well as others.

The *sixth plague* consisted of *boils and blains*; and this also struck at their idolatry in a very remarkable manner. Perhaps our readers will be surprised to hear that in Egypt there were several altars on which they sacrificed *human victims* to the evil principle, or Typhon, or what we would call the devil. So that the devil was one of their gods. Now, the persons who were required to be offered to the Typhon, must be persons of fair complexion and light hair. As the Egyptians were a very dark people, with black hair, it is most likely that the *human victims* which were sacrificed were taken from among the Israelites, for though they were not what we would call persons of fair complexion, yet they were a great deal fairer than the Egyptians. These victims being burned alive, their ashes were gathered together by the priest, and *thrown up* into the air, in order that a blessing might go in whatever direction the ashes were blown. By the direct'on of the Almighty, Moses took a handful of the ashes of the furnace, probably of the very furnace where these victims had been burned, and cast it into the air, and so, instead of a blessing there came a very heavy curse; the *boils and blains*, which were terrible sores, breaking out on man and beast.* This showed that their god, Typhon, could not help his worshippers.

* It should be observed, that this astonishing miracle was wrought in the *sight of Pharaoh*. He saw for himself that light ashes only were thrown up into the air, and that God clothed them with the power to inflict disease and anguish upon the body of the wicked king, and upon all the people of Egypt. It is thought that the ashes came down in the form of dew or rain, and by burning heat produced ulcers or blisters upon the skin. The disease supposed to be the same with the botch of Egypt. Deut. xxviii. 27.

The furnaces, in the labour of which they oppressed the Hebrews, now yielded the instruments of their punishment; for every particle of those ashes, formed by unjust and oppressive labour, seemed to be a boil or a blain on the tyrannic king, and his cruel and hard-hearted people.

The *seventh plague* was that of *lightning and hail*. Like all the others, this was also intended against the idolatry of Egypt, for *Isis* and *Osiris* were worshipped, the first as the god of water, and the other of fire ; and, as lightning and hail are exhibitions of fire and water, it was clearly seen that the God of Israel had them in his control. This plague terrified the Egyptians exceedingly, for we must understand that the sky in Egypt is seldom cloudy, and scarcely any rain falls during the whole year.

The *eighth plague* was that of *locusts ;* and this showed that the Egyptian gods, called *Isis* and *Serapis*, had no power, for they were the gods who were always supposed capable of defending the land from locusts.

The *ninth plague* was that of *darkness*. *Light* was also an object of Egyptian worship, and in this plague it was found that the God of Israel could do with it what he pleased,— even withdraw it from Egypt for three whole days and nights, so that they could not see each other.

All these *nine plagues* were against Egyptian idolatry ; and if we are asked how we know that the great God of Israel—the true God, intended this by it, we have only to repeat what he says about it himself, in Exod. xii. 12 :—" Against *all the gods of Egypt* I will execute judgment. I am the Lord." We also learn that it was to establish his own

G

omnipotent authority, and thus to show the
vanity of all idols and false gods, that all these
things were done; for God also says, " And
the Egyptians shall *know* that I am the LORD,
when I stretch forth my hand upon Egypt."
Exod. vii. 5. And, again, " For I will at this
time send *all my plagues* upon thine heart,
and upon thy servants, and upon thy people,
that *thou mayst know* that there is none *like
me in all the earth.*" Exod. ix. 14.

But there was *one plague*, the *tenth*, which
does not seem to have been against the idolatry of Egypt, but as an act of just recompense
for the murder of the children. " Vengeance
is mine; I will repay saith the Lord." Before this last terrific plague God sent to Pharaoh the following message :—" Thus saith
the Lord, Israel is my son, my first-born.
Let my son go that he may serve me; and if
thou refuse to let him go, behold I will slay thy
son, even thy first-born." Before this threat
was carried into execution, says one, every
effort had been made to subdue the obstinacy
of Pharaoh. Judgment after judgment had
been sent upon him and his people. His gods
were shown to be no gods. His sacred river
was made the source of punishment to him:
the sun refused him its light: the locusts devoured his crops: yet none of these things
succeeded in convincing him that Jehovah
was supreme throughout the universe, and
that it was his wisdom to obey. Then, and

not till then, God raised his arm to strike the terrible blow; and the first-born of Egypt perished in one night.

In all these terrible inflictions but the last, Moses was the instrument in the hand of God; and at his word they came. In this last instance, God sent his destroying angel, who passed through the land of Egypt, and at midnight slew one in every house: a dreadful example of the consequences which must come when sinners harden themselves against the Lord.

CHAPTER X.

The Israelites are sent away in haste.—Their great numbers.—Moses conducts them into the wilderness.—Their arrival at the Red Sea.—Led by the pillar of cloud by day and fire by night.

In our last chapter we went a little beyond the history, because we wanted to consider the plagues of Egypt in one view. Before the last plague, however, which was the destruction of the first-born, God gave Moses some very remarkable directions. Four days before the notice of this last dreadful judgment was given to Pharaoh, God had settled the plan by which the Israelites were to be directed, and Moses gave the people full instruction as to the will of God.

It was ordered that every family, or, in case one family was not large enough, two families joined together, should, on the tenth day of the month, take a lamb, and keep it shut up till the fourteenth day of the month, and then kill it in the afternoon. The lamb was to be a male of the first year, without any blemish. But what was very singular, when it was killed its blood was to be caught in a dish, and then a bunch of hyssop dipped into it, and the blood sprinkled on the side posts of every door, and also on what is called the *lintel*, or top part of the door, and then not one single person was to go outside of the door till they were ordered. Besides this they were to roast the lamb whole, not even breaking one of its bones ; and when it was roasted they were to eat it, with no other dressing than bitter herbs, and no other bread than unleavened bread, or bread made without yeast. And if there was more than was wanted, they were not to carry it away, or give it away, but to burn it with fire. Besides all this they were ordered to eat it, prepared to start off upon a journey— they were to have their garments girded about them, their sandals on their feet, and their staffs or walking sticks ready to take up in a moment; and every thing that was to be carried was to be packed up ready. Now all these were God's directions, and curious as they may seem to us, they all had a very important meaning. We could say much on the subject, but this would not be according to our particular intention, which is the history of Moses. We shall, therefore, content ourselves with giving the reason which God himself has furnished:—" I will *pass through* the land of Egypt this night, and will smite all the first-born in the land of Egypt, both man and beast. And the blood shall be unto you for a token upon the houses where ye are. And when I see the blood, the plague shall not come upon you to destroy you, when I smite the land of Egypt." It was well that the hearts of the Israelites were induced to obey the command of God.

When the appointed day came they slew the lamb; they sprinkled the blood as directed, and at midnight there was a noise of mourning and lamentation throughout the land. In every house it was found that there was one dead.

What a time of distress and terror. It is appalling to our feelings if we hear of the death of one of our friends, but here not one solitary house was there on which the destroying angel had not laid his hand. We cannot even imagine the horror of such a scene. We can form no conception of the cries of anguish and despair. But one thing we can do: we can learn the truth of the declaration, " It is a fearful thing to fall into the hands of the living God." Dear readers, repent and flee to Jesus, for except as his mercy is revealed in Jesus, " our God is a consuming fire."

But let us return to the history. In the middle of the night this dreadful visitation came upon the land of Egypt; and then Pharaoh saw that the God of Israel could no longer be trifled with. Every body was up in the land, probably expecting some other dreadful visitation; and nothing but confusion and distress prevailed. But it was different among the Israelites. The blood on their door posts had been seen by the destroying angel, and at the command of God he had *passed over* the houses of his people. Among the Israelites all was quiet. They were patiently waiting the time of their deliverance; and in the midst of the night they received the king's order to be gone. Moses came back from the king with this cheering message; and not content with now giving them permission to go, both king and people hurried them away. And the more to hasten them, they gave them gold and silver and raiment—they took off their own ornaments to bribe the people to be in haste; and nothing was asked for that was not given them at once.

The Egyptians were so much terrified that they refused nothing; and so much treasure did they heap upon the people, that the history tells us they spoiled the Egyptians.

The Egyptians had gotten their treasures and their costly ornaments from the hard working of the people of God, and what they gave them now was no more than was justly their due for the length and the severity of their labours.

Thus in the midst of the night the Israelites may be said to have been thrust out of Egypt, and they were ready to go, for God in mercy had been long preparing their minds for it, and they had four days to make their arrangements. Before the sun rose upon them they were on their way out of the land where they had been so long held as slaves. They could not but feel that it was the Lord's doing, and it was marvellous in their eyes.

It was in commemoration of this great event that God saw fit to enjoin upon them, as long as they were a people, to keep the feast of the PASSOVER.

Now it was, that Moses came into a situation of great responsibility. No one who was not acting immediately under divine direction would ever have thought of undertaking the task of leading six hundred thousand persons, besides women and children, and a mixed multitude, through a wilderness—for they had no supply of provisions, no arms to fight their foes, and no means to sustain themselves. But God led them, and it was his power that was over them. The whole number probably amounted in all to no less than three millions of persons;

more persons than there are at this moment in the States of New York and Pennsylvania put together. Of all these *Moses* was the *leader;* but God led him, or he never could have sustained the weight of responsibility.

The first day's journey of the people was from Rameses to Succoth, about twelve miles from the land of Goshen, and just on the edge of the wilderness. There was a direct road to the land of Canaan; but God did not see fit to conduct the people that way, because it would have led them through the country of the Philistines, a very brave and warlike people who lived in the southwestern extremity of the land of Canaan, and who would no doubt have attacked them. The people of Israel had, for more than forty years, been unaccustomed to war, they had lived in a state of slavery, and when they left Egypt they had no arms; and though God could and would have protected them, had it been his will that they should go that way, yet we find that he did not often miraculously interpose when any thing could be effected by ordinary means. Therefore, instead of bringing the people to Canaan, through the land of the Philistines, he chose, in his own good pleasure, to lead them another way; through the wilderness unoccupied by any numerous or warlike people.

There is one thing here to be noticed before we go on with the history, which shows how important it is, as long as we live, to remember the requests made by our dying friends. Joseph, when he died in Egypt, had made it one of his dying requests, that when they left Egypt according to God's promise, in which he trusted, they would carry his bones with them, so that they might be buried in the land of promise. When he died, therefore, his body was embalmed and put in a coffin, and kept; and, though his request had been made one hundred and forty-four years before, it was not forgotten. Moses took the bones of Joseph, and carried them along forty years, and at length they were buried with those of his fathers. The dying request of a friend or relative should always be sacred; and it ought never to be neglected unless under circumstances where it would be either impossible or injurious to others. If any of our readers have lost father or mother, who with their dying breath besought them to turn to the Lord and love him, oh! let it not be forgotten, and if it has been neglected until the present time, *now* let it be attended to.

We have already seen that the first place which the Israelites stopped at when they left Egypt was called Succoth. From that place they journeyed to another called Etham, probably not more than twenty miles from Succoth, for it would hardly be possible for a body of people encumbered with baggage, and having a great number of women and children, to travel more than about twenty miles a day.

Connected with the travels of the people

of Israel through the wilderness, there is one of the most extraordinary manifestations of the power and goodness of God which was ever known. The sacred history tells us, that the " Lord went before them' by day in a pillar of a cloud, to lead them in the way, and by night in a pillar of fire to give them light; to go by day and by night." And this wonderful appearance continued as long as there was any difficulty in finding their way. In that pillar the Lord went with them. It was what we call a symbol, or sign, or representation of the *presence* of God, and therefore it was a continued proof that God was with them.

It is here that we may remark the care and kindness of God to his ancient people. Every one knows that there was a necessity for some guide to direct them through the wilderness, even though they had been permitted to take the most easy and direct road, how much more so when they took a *circuitous,* or what we would call a roundabout way, which none would ever have thought of travelling except guided by some supernatural means. It is very probable that Moses himself knew nothing about the way: that he neither knew when or where they were to stop or to go, but depended entirely on the Divine direction. It is supposed that this PILLAR, in which God went as their invisible leader, was intended, in his mercy, to answer a great variety of purposes. In the day time it was merely a cloud, which was quite sufficient, for all the people could see it. In the night it assumed the appearance of *fire*, which gave them always as much light as they needed. But, besides this, in the day time, it answered the purpose of a *shade*, for in that dreadfully hot climate it would have been almost impossible for the women and children to march during the day time, exposed to the burning sun; and hence we have good reason to suppose that the *cloud* which led them was also a *shadow from the heat*. We do not like, however, to assert any thing of this kind, unless we can find something in the Scripture which seems to justify our opinions. Paul, in his first epistle to the Corinthians, x. 1, alluding to the passage through the wilderness, says, " Moreover, brethren, I would not that ye should be ignorant how that all our fathers were *under* the cloud;" and David, in the Psalms, says, certainly, " He spread a cloud for a *covering*, and fire to give light in the night." How wonderfully was the goodness of God displayed, and it is just so with all who love him. In some way or other he will see fit to bless and protect them. Only love the Lord and all shall be well.

The last encampment of the children of Israel which we noticed was at Etham. Moses was now directed to lead the people towards the Red Sea. They were to encamp before a place called Pi-hahiroth, which may mean the mouth or bay of *Chiroth*, between *Migdol*, which was probably a tower or fort to defend the bay and the sea, opposite to a place called *Baal-zephon*, supposed to have been either an idol temple, or something intended to answer the purpose of our lighthouses. It is not possible to fix exactly upon the position of these places, and therefore we do not pretend to state any thing about them with certainty. Such very great changes have taken place in so many hundred years, that no one can do much more than make a probable conjecture. The best idea of the situation will be gathered by consulting the map which we have had carefully prepared from the best authorities.

God gave to Moses a very singular reason for ordering the people to encamp at this place :—" For Pharaoh will say of the children of Israel, They *are* entangled in the land, the wilderness hath shut them in. And I will harden Pharaoh's heart, that he should follow after them ; and I will be honoured upon Pharaoh, and upon all his host ; that the Egyptians may know that I *am* the LORD, And they did so." Ex. xiv. 3, 4. To this place, then, they were led, and here we shall leave them, while we go back a little in the history to see how Pharaoh and the Egyptians bore the departure of the children of Israel.

CHAPTER XI.

Pharaoh repents of having let the people go.—
Pursues the Israelites.—Overtakes them,
but is kept from hurting them.—The Is-
raelites pass over the Red Sea.—Pharaoh
attempts to do it and is drowned, he and his
hosts.

We have seen that under the alarm which
was occasioned by the death of the first-born
of every family in Egypt, Pharaoh and his
people were induced to let the people of Israel go. But as soon as they recovered a
little from their fright, all their evil passions
seem to have revived, just as is usually the
case with sinners. In seasons of affliction
they make many excellent promises and resolutions, but no sooner does the affliction pass
away, than these are forgotten, and they are
as bad or worse than before.

Pharaoh appears to have been much displeased with himself for having let the people
go; and when some persons who had gone
with the Israelites, very probably as spies,
returned to Egypt, and told him that the Israelites were likely to flee away so that he
never would recover them, his pride, and his
avarice, and his hatred of the people, resumed
their sway over his heart. He determined at
all hazards to bring them back to a state of

H

slavery, for he found their services too profitable to be willing to part with them. Pharaoh and his people all seem to have united in saying, " Why have we done this, to let Israel go from serving us;" as if they had said, " What fools we have been to be so frightened, and thus lose our slaves. We shall now have to do our work for ourselves. Let us go and bring them back again." In consequence of this foolhardy determination, Pharaoh made ready his chariots and horsemen. We are told that he " took six hundred chosen chariots, and all the chariots of Egypt, and captains over every one of them." And with this mighty military force he overtook the people at the place of their encampment near the Red Sea. This was a situation which seemed to make escape impossible for the Israelites. Before them lay the Red Sea, which at this place is supposed to have been no less than twelve miles wide; on their right hand and on their left were high and impassable mountains with forts or towers on their tops; and behind them was the whole military power of Egypt, led on by the king, thirsting for vengeance, and determined to bring them back to slavery, or to slay them with swords and spears and his chariots armed with scythes. They knew that flight was impossible, and resistance in vain; for, besides their not being accustomed to war, they had no weapons, so that without the divine interference they had nothing to expect but immediate destruction.

In this dreadful posture of affairs, the whole body of the Israelites were alarmed and terrified. Some cried unto the Lord, we are afraid not with the prayer of faith, but with somewhat of the same feelings which agitated the bosom of the servant of the prophet, whom we read of in 2 Kings vi. 15, who, when he saw the chariots and horsemen of the king of Syria surrounding the walls of Dothan, cried out, " Alas, my master, what shall we do?" But there were others who did nothing but try to vent their fury upon Moses in such reproachful language as this :—" Because there were no graves in Egypt hast thou taken us away to die in the wilderness? wherefore hast thou dealt thus with us, to carry us forth out of Egypt? Is not this the word we did tell thee, saying, Let us alone ; for it had been better for us to serve the Egyptians than that we should die in the wilderness?" This language was as foolish as it was sinful. Who was Moses that they should murmur against him? says a writer. Had he not acted throughout by the divine direction? Had he not equally with them hazarded every thing that was dear? Had they forgotten what wonderful and mighty works the Lord had wrought to rescue them from their bondage? or why should they distrust his care? Had they not before them the visible tokens of his presence, the pillar of the

cloud? Alas! we perceive in them a picture
of ourselves. How soon do we lose the remembrance of past deliverances! Every fresh
danger awakens our fear, as if we had known
nothing of the goodness of the Lord.

In this trying state of affairs, when his feelings must have been very much hurt by the
reproaches of those whom he was most zealously trying to serve, Moses did not lose his
trust in the Lord. He did not answer the
people with any reproachful language: he
maintained his meek and patient spirit; and
with the utmost *faith* in God, he tried to
quiet the fears of the people, by saying,
" Fear ye not, stand still and see the salvation
of the Lord which he will show you to-day;
for the Egyptians whom ye have seen to-day,
ye shall see them again no more for ever.
The Lord shall fight for you, and you shall
hold your peace." This declaration, made in
faith, was made good to the very letter, as we
shall soon see.

In the midst of all the confusion made by
the approach of the Egyptians, and the alarms
and reproaches of the Israelites, Moses had
no opportunity to retire to pray to God for
direction, but he did *pray in his heart,* and
the Lord heard him. No mention is made of
his praying, but his spirit was wrestling in
supplication with the Most High, as Hannah
prayed in her heart, while her voice was not
heard by Eli. The Lord regarded this silent

prayer of Moses, and says unto him, " Wherefore criest thou unto me : speak to the children
of Israel that they go forward." Was there
ever a more strange and singular order given :
" Go forward,"—march through the sea,
twelve miles wide, and deep enough to drown
ten thousand times their number. But God
commanded, and God provided the means of
obedience ; and here, though it may interrupt
the history for a moment, we feel bound to
give a word of advice and encouragement.
God never makes a command which he is not
able and willing, in some way, to enable you
to obey. Remember the case of the man
with a withered hand, as the story is told in
the New Testament. Was the command at
all easier for him to obey, " stretch out thine
hand," than it was for the Israelites to march
through the Red Sea? No: his hand was
palsied and dead. Yet the cripple felt that
an attempt at least was due to the authority
of him who had given the order. He accord-
ingly made the effort, and it was followed by
a blessing : " his arm was restored whole as
the other." So it is with all. No matter
what difficulties are in the way of duty to
God, " Go forward." *Duties* are with you,
events are with God. You have no right
either to hesitate in duty, or to doubt in difficulty : " you can do all things through Christ
who strengtheneth you." His power will
go before you, and hindrances will disappear.

No sooner had God told Moses to speak to the children of Israel that they should go forward, than he takes away all the difficulties at once, by telling him to take his rod in his hand, and to stretch it out, over the sea, and divide the waters, and that they should all go through on dry land. God also tells Moses that the time for Pharaoh's entire overthrow was now come. That his heart would be hardened, so that he would even pursue the Israelites into the midst of the sea, and there perish, a terrible monument of the folly of fighting against God.

But how does it happen that the Egyptians did not attack the Israelites before this was done ? Here we see the goodness and mercy of God to his people. No sooner did the immense army of the Egyptians come near the camp of the Israelites, than the Lord, who guided them, removed the pillar of the cloud, and instead of going before them it went *behind* them, just between the Egyptians and them ; and we are told that while one side of it was all bright, and gave light to the Israelites, the other side, which was towards the Egyptians, was so dark that they could not see to get near the people of God, and this continued till they were safely over the sea. But, in the meantime, Moses, according to the command of God, had stretched forth his hand, and then the Lord brought a very strong east wind all that night, and by his almighty power the waters, instead of running on in the usual course, stood, just like a wall, on the right hand and the left, leaving a dry space in the middle large enough for the immense body of the Israelites to go through. As soon as Moses perceived that the water was thus forming a wall, he ordered the people to move on, which they did all night, lighted by the pillar of fire which stood between them and the Egyptians, and which turned its bright side towards them alone.

The Egyptians, infatuated and blinded by their sinful passions, pushed on, and pursued the Israelites right into the passage which the power of God had made; and they were now in the situation of those spoken of by Solomon, when he says, " he that being oft reproved hardeneth his neck, shall suddenly be destroyed, and that without remedy." About daylight the next morning, when the Israelites were all safely landed on the south side of the Red Sea, and while the whole Egyptian army were in the midst of the sea, then the Lord brought ruin upon them. To prevent their overtaking the people of Israel, in some miraculous manner, the wheels of their chariots came off, and they then dragged them along with great difficulty; and then they began to think, when it was too late, that they had brought themselves into ruin. " Let us flee," said they, " from the face of Israel, for the Lord fighteth for them against the Egyptians."

What a pity it was that they had not learned
that lesson before ; for there was quite enough
to teach them, but now it was too late.   They
had resisted and fought against God till the
cup of their iniquity was full, and God tells
Moses :—" Stretch out thine hand over the
sea, that the waters may come again."   Moses
did as he was commanded—the waters came
into their place, and in a very few moments
Pharaoh and his hosts—his chosen chariots
and captains, and his deluded people, were *all*
of them drowned.   Not one was left, so total
was the destruction which had come upon
them for their rebellion against God.   And
thus it was that the Lord saved the people of
Israel out of the hands of enemies who had

been for a great number of years persecuting them, and plotting their destruction. When the people, thus redeemed by the mighty hand of God, stood on the shore, and saw what was done in their behalf, we are told that they feared the Lord, and his servant Moses. The experience of almighty power and boundless mercy, for a little time banished their infidelity and rebellion.

This portion of the history is most useful to us, as it points out the difference which God puts between the righteous and the wicked. The faithful and obedient servants of Jesus Christ, may pass through difficulties, be exercised by trial, be weak in faith, be bowed down by despondency, but they " go forward." The waters of affliction, instead of going over their heads, to overwhelm them, are made the means of their benefit, until at length they have crossed the sea which divides time and eternity, and shout hallelujah for victory through their Redeemer. But it is not so with the wicked. They oppose the Lord, but they bring upon themselves nothing but ruin. Pharaoh found it so; the inhabitants of the world before the flood found it so; other sinners have found it so, and all sinners will at last find it so. Now, then, is the time to repent and turn to God. The Egyptians would have been glad enough to fly when the waters of the Red Sea began to return upon them; and gladly would impenitent sinners fly to Christ when the judgment of the great day comes upon them. But then it will be too late. The Egyptians perished to a man : not one was left. And, so, the destruction of impenitent sinners will be universal and eternal. Are there any such among the readers of this little volume, oh, let them resist the Lord no longer. Let them flee to Christ. Escape is *now* possible, but soon it will be too late. "To-day, while it is called to-day, harden not your hearts."

CHAPTER XII.

Moses composes a song of victory, which the people sing.—The journey continued.— Murmuring at Marah.—A tree cast into bitter waters makes them sweet.—Elim.— Quails and manna sent for food.—Murmuring at Massah and Meribah.—Moses ordered to smite the rock for water.—War with the Amalekites.—And visit of Jethro.

In our last chapter we gave an account of the wonderful dealings of God with the people of Israel, in opening a passage for them through the Red Sea, and delivering them for ever from the long-continued cruelty of the Egyptians. No sooner had they recovered

from the wonder into which they were thrown
by these great events, than a day was set apart
as a solemn thanksgiving to God for their
marvellous deliverance. On this occasion
Moses composed an anthem, or sacred song,
to commemorate the event, and to show forth
the glory of God. That song is contained at
length in the fifteenth chapter of Exodus, and
is the very first song of victory which we find
recorded in the Scriptures. Although it reads
just as the other parts of Scripture, yet it is
highly poetical in its character, and full of
the loftiest expressions of the power and greatness of Jehovah. We cannot here quote the
song, but we have a piece of poetry, which
we believe has never been published in this
country, and which beautifully gives the sense
of this song of Moses :—

" Our slavery is finished, our labour is done ;
   Our tasks are relinquish'd, our march is begun :
   The arm of the Lord has divided the sea,
   JEHOVAH has conquered, and Israel is free.

" ' Why stay ye the fast-going chariots ? and why
   Is the far-floating banner uplifted on high ?
   Quick, quick ! let the corselets your bosoms embrace ;
   And harness the courser, and hasten the chase !'

" Thus Pharaoh has spoke in the storm of his pride,
   And roll'd on our footsteps his numberless tide ;
   The falchions are bright in the hands of the foe,
   Their quivers are rattling, and bent is each bow.

"As the clouds of the tempest, which gloomily frown,
   That wide-spreading band in the evening comes down ,
   As the thunder-cloud bursts at the sun's piercing ray,
   That band on the morrow shall vanish away.

" Proud boaster of Egypt! be silent and mourn;
  Weep, daughter of Memphis, thy banner is torn;
  In the temple of Isis be wailing and wo,
  For the mighty are fallen, and princes laid low.

" Their chieftains are fall'n though their bows were still
    bent;
  Their legions are sunk, though their shafts were un-
    spent;
  The horse and his rider are whelmed in the sea;
  JEHOVAH has conquered, and Israel is free!"

After spending this day of thanksgiving, they again set off on their march; and they had to go three days' journey before they came to any place where there was water. In those countries, persons who travel carry as much water as possible with them; but it appears that such an immense body as the Israelites could not have carried water enough to last more than three days. At this time, therefore, they reached a stream, but we may judge of their disappointment when we find that as soon as they tasted it they discovered it was bitter, or what we would call *brackish* or *saltish*; that is, the water had a strong taste of salt, like seawater, and every one who has ever tasted this knows that it is very disagreeable. The Israelites had been used to drinking the very best water which the world afforded, namely, that of the river Nile, and we need not wonder if their taste was somewhat spoiled; just as a child who had been indulged with cakes all his life, would find it hard to make a hearty meal from a piece of coarse rye bread. But if in the providence of God, one, who had been indulged with cakes, should be obliged to make his dinner upon a hard brown loaf, there would be no reason why he should murmur; for perhaps the brown loaf would be much better than he deserved, and at all events every one ought to be thankful for whatever he gets, and learn, like the good apostle, " in whatsoever state he is, therewith to be content." So, because God brought the Israelites where there was not any such good water as they had been accustomed to drink, it was no excuse for the sin of murmuring, and that, too, only three days after God had so signally interposed in their behalf in the wonderful passage of the Red Sea. But those whose hearts are not right with God are never truly grateful. God, however, who is rich in mercy, here also interposed in their behalf. When Moses went for direction, in relation to these bitter waters, God showed him a tree, and told him to cast it into the waters. This he did, and the waters became immediately sweet, not that the tree itself had any power of making the waters sweet, but this was the way in which God saw fit to change the taste of the waters. The tree derived all its virtue from the power of almighty God: from the fulness of his blessing upon the means which he had revealed and ,commanded to be employed. So no earthly consolations can ever change affliction

I

into joy, but God can do it, and will do it when with patient submission to his will, we look to him for help. The place where these things occurred to the Israelites was called *Marah*, because this word signifies *bitter*.

From *Marah* they marched on to *Elim*, a place where they found *twelve* wells of water which was good. They also found there three score and ten, or seventy palm trees, and they encamped in this pleasant place.

It is a little singular that the number of wells corresponded exactly with the number of tribes, so that each tribe may have had a well to itself, and thus there was no confusion.

God was very merciful in bringing them into a place where there was so many palm trees also, for the palm tree of the East bears a very good fruit, called *dates*. The palm tree grows very beautifully, and to a great height, perfectly straight. It is for this reason that an upright man is compared to it in the Scriptures :—" The righteous shall flourish like the *palm tree*." A traveller, who went through this same country many hundred years after Moses and the people of Israel, stopped there, says, " I saw no more than nine of the twelve wells mentioned by Moses, the other three being filled up with sand ; yet this loss is amply made up by the great increase of palm trees, the seventy having propagated themselves into more than two thousand."

The next place which is mentioned, as an encampment of the children of Israel, is the *Wilderness of Sin*. This lies between Elim and Mount Sinai. This place they reached on the fifteenth day of the second month after they left Egypt: thus they had been travelling just one month. Here we find them murmuring for bread, and by and by for meat, so discontented is human nature. The first time that any murmuring is recorded, namely at Marah, it is supposed that but few were engaged in it, but now we are told that the whole congregation murmured. All cry out for bread and for meat. " Would to God," say they, " we had died in Egypt;" and then they ungratefully turned upon Moses and Aaron, and said, " Ye have brought us forth into this wilderness to kill us with hunger." Their murmurings were apparently against Moses and Aaron, but all such discontents are actually against God, and so Moses told them. "What are *we*, your murmurings are not against us, but against the Lord." Once more God forgave their murmurings, and supplied their wants. He caused immense flocks of quails to come up every evening, and showers of manna to fall every night. This manna was a very curious thing, and something which we do not exactly know how to describe ; for what we now call manna, which is used as a medicine, is not at all the same thing. It is said to have been a small round thing, as small as the hoar frost; that is, white frost, which we see on the ground in the fall and spring of the year. And again we are told, in Numbers, that the manna " was as coriander seed, and the colour thereof as bdellium," that is, a kind of pearl colour, or nearly white and transparent. It was always preceded or accompanied by a copious dew; and when that went off, which it always does when the sun rises, then the manna became visible, and was gathered in great quantities; an *omer*, or about five or six pints for each person.

What an immense quantity must have fallen then, to have fed nearly three millions of people. And what was very curious about it was, that the people were never to gather more than enough to last them one day, except on the day before the Sabbath, when they were to gather enough for two days; and it so happened that if the people on any other week day, except the day before the Sabbath, gathered more than a certain quantity, it always bred worms, and became very offensive to the smell; but the quantity which they gathered on the day before the Sabbath never bred worms, nor became offensive.

No doubt by this arrangement God intended to answer two great purposes. He meant by sending food every day, to teach them the lesson of continual dependence upon him; and by requiring them to gather twice as much on the day before the Sabbath, he showed that he meant them to keep holy the Sabbath day, and this was before the fourth command. ment was given.

We have not room in this history, to dwell on all the minute circumstances which are recorded of the Israelites in their journey through the wilderness. Though we cannot always avoid it, yet we do not wish to go further in the history than may be necessary to display the character of Moses. The ingratitude of the people, their dreadful stubbornness, their unbelief, their murmurings, and rebellion, are very strikingly contrasted with the meekness and patience of Moses.

From the Wilderness of Sin, the Israelites were led by the cloudy pillar to a place called Rephidim. Here again they experienced a scarcity of water, and here again they murmured against Moses and against the Lord; and indeed their rage rose to so great a pitch, that they came near to stone Moses to death. It was on this occasion that he was directed to take his rod in his hand, and to smite a certain rock in Horeb; and on his doing it, it poured out a clear and delightful stream of water, which went along with the Israelites during most of their journey. There is a rock which travellers see to this day, and which they suppose to be the one smitten by Moses. It is of that kind of stone which they call red granite; about twelve or fifteen feet square; with several holes and channels, which appear to have been formed by the bursting of running water.

This stream doubtless supplied them for a considerable time; hence it was said, figuratively, that the rock followed them. And as it was customary in those early times, to record events by giving names, this place, Rephidim, was called *Massah*, "temptation," because here they tempted God; and *Meribah*, "chiding," or strife, because here they chided Moses. This rock, which by being wounded produced a copious stream of water, is also represented by the apostle Paul, as typical of Christ. "They drank of that spiritual Rock that followed them" in a stream of living water, and "that Rock was Christ," (1 Cor. x. 4.)

On this circumstance one piously remarks, that " Christ (the spiritual Rock) being smitten by the rod of Moses, and bearing the curse of the law for our sins, from him floweth that spiritual drink wherewith all believers are refreshed." (See John xix. 34. 1 John ver. 8.)

One difficulty, however, was scarcely surmounted, when another came up. While they were at Rephidim, little expecting such an event, the king of the Amalekites, at the head of a large number of his people, came and attacked the Israelites. This attack was a very mean and cowardly one, for they came to the rear of the camp, and fell to killing and plundering those in the rear: probably the women and children, the sick and weary. It is very likely that like the wandering Arabs in the same country at the present day, their object was rather plunder than any thing else; but in order to plunder they did not care whom they killed.

Moses, however, was ready as soon as the difficulty was understood, and he chose a young man, Joshua, to be the captain; and all things were prepared to give battle to the Amalekites. On the next day, the Amalekites came on again, and Joshua went out to meet them. But what was Moses doing? Ah, Moses did what was as good as fighting: he went up to the top of a hill, with his rod in his hand, where he could see the battle, and there he lifted up his hands in

prayer to God, that he would fight for them.
And just so long as Moses held up his hands
in prayer the Israelites prevailed, and when
he ceased praying their enemies prevailed.

As the battle was a very long one, for it
lasted all day, Moses, from his age and excitement of mind, grew weary. It was happy
that Aaron and Hur were with him, for they
brought him a stone to set upon, and they as-
sisted in holding up his hands, so that about
sun-down the victory declared for Joshua and
the people; and the Amalekites were defeated
and driven off.

This was the first time we read of Joshua.
He afterwards became very distinguished.
And this was the first battle which the Israelites ever had. We do not know how many
were killed; but it must have been a dreadful
battle. God told Moses to write an account
of it, for the purpose of guiding Joshua in his
future conduct towards the Amalekites, which
he did; and, to commemorate the goodness of
the Lord, he built an altar on the very place
where he had sat, and called it Jehovah Nissi,
the Lord my Banner.

One very interesting circumstance here took
place, in relation to Moses himself. While
they were at this place, *Rephidim*, he had a
visit from his father-in-law, Jethro. It appears that Zipporah, who it will be remembered was the wife of Moses, for some reason
not clearly expressed, left Moses on his entering

into Egypt, and went back to her father; but here returning with Jethro, and with both her children, is cordially received. Before Jethro arrives, however, he " said unto Moses," doubtless by the hand of a messenger, " I am come unto thee: and Moses went out to meet him." Jethro, both by this and by his subsequent conduct, appears to have been a wise and prudent man, and a worshipper of Jehovah; for he " rejoiced in all the goodness which Jehovah had done to Israel," and acknowledged him to be, if *not* the *only*, yet the *supreme* God; for he said, " Now I know that Jehovah is greater than all gods." Jethro appears to have been a priest of the patriarchal order, and therefore united with Moses and Aaron, and the elders of Israel, in a sacrificial feast. But his wisdom particularly appears in the advice which he subsequently gave to Moses, to appoint certain elders of the people to assist him in determining all petty controversies, which, among so discontented a people, were doubtless very numerous, and would soon wear out the strength of a younger man than Moses. " There may be over-doing (says Mr. Henry) in well-doing; and therefore our zeal must always be governed by discretion, that our good may not be evil spoken of. Wisdom is profitable to direct, that we may neither content ourselves with less than our duty, nor overtask ourselves with that which is beyond our strength."

Moses, however, following his advice, established an excellent system of courts, by means of elders chosen from the people, with an appeal to himself in the last resort, and in all cases of peculiar difficulty. In nothing, however, is the wisdom of Jethro more apparent, than in the characters he advises Moses to select; " able men, such as fear God, men of truth, hating covetousness ;" and they were to " judge the people at all seasons ;" thus securing all the important objects of a good government, a wise and impartial judgment, promptly administered ; for nothing tends more to the increase of crime, than the delay and uncertainty of justice. It is " because sentence is not executed speedily, that the hearts of the sons of men are fully set in them to do evil." Eccles. viii. 11.

Jethro also shows his independence of mind and disinterestedness, in immediately returning to his own country, without stopping to fill any one of those high departments, to which his talents and character would certainly have entitled him. Of Zipporah we hear little more ; it is possible she did not long survive ; if she did, her attention was wisely and prudently confined to her family and domestic concerns.

CHAPTER XIII.

Preparations for giving the Law on Mount Sinai.—Glorious appearance of the presence of God.—The law of the Ten Commandments given by God himself.

WE have now arrived at a portion of the history of Moses, which is connected with some of the most extraordinary events which ever took place on earth. We mean the giving the law on Mount Sinai. In writing the life of Moses, we of course cannot enter into the meaning of those laws and institutions which God then delivered. We propose to go no further than to show how, in the wisdom of God, Moses was connected with them. We trust that every reader of this little volume is acquainted with the Ten Commandments; and it would be a most glorious and happy thing, if every one made them a rule by which he would seek to govern his conduct, for they embrace every duty which we owe to God or to man; so that our Saviour has most justly represented them, when he said, " Thou shalt love the Lord thy God with all thy heart, and with all thy soul, and with all thy mind. This is the first and great commandment.

And the second is like unto it, Thou shalt love thy neighbour as thyself. On these two commandments hang all the law and the prophets." Matt. xxii. 37—40.

We learn from the sacred history that, under the leading of Moses, the people of Israel came to the wilderness of Sinai in the third month, and most probably the first day of the month. This is generally supposed to be the forty-sixth day after they left the land of Egypt.

The wilderness of Sinai is a large plain, nearly nine miles long and three broad. It is open on the north east, but completely closed on the south by the mountain itself. This mountain has two peaks or summits, one is called Horeb, and the other Sinai; but it is probable that originally they had but one name, and were both called Horeb. By looking on the map, it will be seen that this mountain stands at the south corner of the point of land which runs into the Red Sea, and which separates between the gulf of Colzum on the west, and what is called the Elanitic gulf on the east. It has never been exactly ascertained how high Mount Sinai is, but as its top is covered with snow all the year, in the burning climate of Arabia, it can hardly be supposed to be less than ten thousand feet.

The Israelites were encamped at the foot of this range of mountains for nearly a year; and it was during this time, that God delivered the

law, and a great variety of orders which related to the civil and ecclesiastical condition
of the people.

In order to prepare the minds of the people
for the reception of the law, and to impress
them with reverence for his own character,
God saw fit to introduce the giving of the law
by circumstances of the most striking and
awful solemnity.

In the first place God told Moses what he
was about to do, and directed him to address
the people, and require of them three days
special spiritual preparation. They were to
be sanctified, or separated for this purpose,
and in token of their inward purification they
were to wash their clothes. They were also
to spend the intervening time in fasting and
prayer, and on the third day gather themselves round about the foot of the mount.
But in order to keep them at a proper distance
bounds were set, which none were to pass
under the penalty of death.

All things being thus prepared, on the third
day, which was now the fiftieth after their departure from Egypt, the solemn transactions,
which God had previously spoken of, began
to take place. On the top of Mount Sinai
there was a thick cloud gathered, and out of
that cloud they saw the most vivid flashes of
lightning, and heard the most appalling thun-
der; and besides this there was the sound of
a trumpet so exceedingly loud, that every one

K

of the people trembled for fear. Even Moses himself, as Paul tells us in the epistle to the Hebrews, was constrained to say, " I exceedingly fear and quake." While the trumpet was sounding, long and loud, Moses brought the people out of their tents, and ranged them round the mountain as God had commanded. Then the whole mountain appeared, as it were, filled with smoke, as if from a burning furnace; for the great God descended upon it, in fire, and the mountain trembled as if it would be entirely destroyed. The trumpet continued to sound louder and louder, and at last a voice, which was the voice of God, called Moses up into the mount. According to command Moses went up, and received a message to go down and prevent the people from encroaching on the boundaries which had been set. Moses went down and addressed the people, and then God spake in a voice which could be heard by every individual surrounding the mountain, and delivered those commands which we call the *Decalogue*, or the Ten Commandments.

We cannot well imagine the solemn awe and terror which this scene must have wrought in the minds of the people of Israel. To have the great Jehovah speak to them in a voice which all could hear and understand; to hear commands so pure and holy; and to have it all accompanied by thunderings and lightnings, and the sound of a trumpet loud and long; to feel the earth shaking beneath them, and to see the mountain apparently burning up—all this was enough to awaken their terrors; and we are not surprised to find that they removed from the bottom of the mount, and stood at a distance gazing on the solemn and terrific scene. They then said to Moses, " speak thou with us, and we will hear; but let not God speak with us lest we die."

Moses endeavoured to encourage them, and told them that they need not fear; that God was come to prove them; and that all this terror was to impress upon their minds the awful danger of sinning against God. Moses, however, did as they desired, and he *alone* drew near to the burning mountain, and the thick darkness where God had hid his presence from all human gaze. There God talked with him, and gave him those directions which are recorded in the latter part of the twentieth chapter, and continued through the 21st, 22d, and 23d chapters of Exodus. And thus closed the most solemn day, and the most solemn and important transactions which ever occurred on earth, if we except the great transactions of Calvary's sacred mountain; when our Lord, Jesus Christ, gave himself up as an offering and sacrifice for sin. And never, till the light of the last morning shall dawn upon the world, and the archangel's trumpet shall sound its summons to arouse the dead, and to bring all mankind before the judgment seat of Christ, and receive their eternal destiny—never, until the last great fire shall burn up the earth, and all that is therein, will there be such a spectacle as was this day exhibited to the men of Israel, while they stood round Mount Sinai, and received the law.

The law of God, every one of us has broken. How then are we to escape, and where are we to look? The gospel of our Saviour answers these questions. It tells us, that the " Law is a schoolmaster to bring us unto Christ that we may be justified by faith." The law does this, by showing the convinced transgressor plainly to himself as exposed to the wrath of a sin-hating God. It compels him to ask, " What shall I do to be saved." The sinner looks back to Sinai, and he hears " Cursed is every one who continueth not in all things written in the book of the law to do them." He looks forward to the gospel; he sees the cross of Calvary; he hears the precious invitation :—" Believe in the Lord Jesus Christ, and thou shalt be saved." He then finds that he can neither perform the perfect conditions of the law, nor endure the penalty of transgression. In this state the Holy Spirit convinces him of sin; takes of the things of Christ, and shows them unto him. He looks into the gospel, and reads, " Christ hath redeemed us from the curse of the law, being made a curse for us." Gal. iii. 13. " In whom we have redemption through his blood, the forgiveness of sin, according to the riches of his grace." Ephes. i. 7. "And by him all that believe are justified from all things," &c. Acts xiii. 39.

The more, indeed, we know of the law, and the more we become acquainted with ourselves, the more directly and speedily shall we be induced to flee to the reconciling mercy of God in Jesus Christ, and submit ourselves to him; and we shall seek to be found in him, not having our own righteousness, which is of the law, but that which is through the faith of Christ, the righteousness which is of God by faith.

Dear readers, consider your privileges as those who live under the gospel covenant. How beautifully Paul contrasts your situation with that of those who were without the full revelation of the gospel:—" For ye are not come unto the mount that might be touched, and that burned with fire, nor unto blackness, and darkness, and tempest, and the sound of a trumpet, and the voice of words: which voice they that heard, entreated that the word should not be spoken to them any more: (For they could not endure that which was commanded, And if so much as a beast touch the mountain, it shall be stoned, or thrust through with a dart: and so terrible was the sight, that Moses said, I exceedingly fear and quake:) But ye are come unto mount Sion, and unto

K 2

the city of the living God, the heavenly Jeru-
salem, and to an innumerable company of
angels, to the general assembly and church
of the first-born, which are written in heaven,
and to God the judge of all, and to the spirits
of just men made perfect, and to Jesus the
mediator of the new covenant, and to the
blood of sprinkling, that speaketh better things
than that of Abel." Heb. xii. 18—24. A
trumpet, indeed, is sounding, but it is not the
loud and terrible trumpet of Sinai. It is the
silver trumpet of the gospel jubilee which
proclaims pardon, peace, life, love, holiness,
and heaven.

But superior privileges imply superior responsibility :—" See that ye refuse not him
that speaketh. For if they escaped not who
refused him that spake on earth, much more
shall not we escape, if we turn away from him
that speaketh from heaven : Whose voice then
shook the earth: but now he hath promised,
saying, Yet once more I shake not the earth
only, but also heaven. And this word, Yet
once more, signifies the removing of those
things that are shaken, as of things that are
made, that those things which cannot be
shaken may remain. Wherefore we receiving
a kingdom which cannot be moved, let us
have grace, whereby we may serve God ac-
ceptably with reverence and godly fear. For
our God is a consuming fire." Heb. xii.
25—29.

CHAPTER XIV.

Moses is called up into the Mount, and there remains with God forty days and forty nights.—How occupied during this time. —The people of Israel worship the golden calf.—Aaron also guilty.—God informs Moses of the transaction, and orders him to return to the people.—Moses breaks the tables of the law.

WHEN Moses had finished instructing the people in those laws which were given him after the solemn announcement of the Ten Commandments, which God had himself spoken to the people, he was summoned to return to the mount, and to take with him *Aaron, Nadab,* and *Abihu,* and *seventy* of the elders of the children of Israel. These persons were to remain on the mount, while Moses alone was permitted to draw near to the immediate presence of God. Previous to this, however, Moses again addressed himself to the people, and told them all that God had communicated to him. The people testified their entire willingness to obey the commands of the Lord. After this Moses wrote all that God had commanded him; and after a solemn sacrifice, where he and the people entered into a covenant of agreement with God, he read the book he had prepared to all the people, and they again professed their determination of obedience. He then took the blood of the sacrifice, and sprinkled it half on the people and half on the altar, calling it " the blood of the covenant which the Lord had made with them." This whole circumstance was, no doubt, intended to impress on their minds one of the most important truths to which their attention could be directed, viz., that the covenant was made with them only through the blood of an atoning sacrifice. This, the apostle tells us, in Heb. ix. 18—23, was intended as a shadow or type of the manner in which all true believers are admitted into covenant with God, that is, through the atoning sacrifice of our Lord and Saviour Jesus Christ.

When this solemn transaction was over, Moses, Aaron, Nadab, and Abihu, and the seventy elders, went up into the mount, and there, as representatives of the people, they were permitted to have a view of the glory of God, of a character totally different from that which had just before been exhibited. When God gave the law he appeared in the *terrors of* his majesty, here he appears under an aspect of peculiar *mildness*. It is supposed that these two representations are intended to be symbolical of the character of God, in the two aspects under which he has seen fit to reveal himself to men. In the law he appears as a consuming fire, requiring perfect and unsinning obedience. In the gospel he appears in all the mild radiance of his character, as in Jesus Christ, willing to forgive sin, and receive the sinner into favour, when he repents and turns to Jesus. As to the appearance of the glory of God here spoken of, we can only describe it in the language of the Scriptures, for to add any thing would but show our own folly and presumption. " And they saw the God of Israel: and there was under his feet as it were a paved work of a sapphire stone, and as it were the body of heaven in his clearness." Ex. xxiv. 10.

After this striking circumstance, Moses, being called of God, took Joshua with him, and went up higher into the mount. Here they remained six days, no doubt in holy prayer and contemplation; and on the seventh day God called Moses again, and then, leaving Joshua, he went still higher on the mount, and being surrounded by the glory of the Lord, which to the people who were below looked like devouring fire, there, in the immediate presence of God, he remained forty days and forty nights. During this time his body was sustained by miracle, as God rendered it unnecessary for him to have his accustomed food; just as afterwards Elijah, and, still later, our blessed Saviour, during the period of his temptation, fasted forty days, and were miraculously sustained.

The sacred history lets us into a knowledge of what was done during these forty days and nights when Moses was in the mount with God. Here he was instructed as to the building of a tabernacle, and every minute circumstance connected with it; here he was directed as to the appointment of a regular priesthood, which was to be confined to Aaron and his sons, and all the ceremonies and offerings which were to be connected with the service; here also Moses was instructed as to the persons who were to be engaged in the building of the tabernacle. All these directions are contained in the chapters of the book of Exodus, beginning with the twenty-fifth and ending with the thirty-first. As the description of the tabernacle, with its rich and costly furniture, its uses, its priests, its sacrifices, and its symbolical character, belongs rather to the history of the Jewish people than to the history of Moses, we are compelled to pass over it unnoticed. It would make a most deeply interesting and valuable book, but would swell the history far beyond the limits assigned to the present work. In the meantime we will direct the attention of our readers, who are desirous of further information, to a work published by the AMERICAN SUNDAY-SCHOOL UNION, called " *Biblical Antiquities;*" where the whole history of the tabernacle is largely treated.

At the close of the interesting communication which God held with Moses during these forty days and forty nights, he gave him two tablets of stone, on which he himself had written the Ten Commandments; hence said, in the language of the Scripture, to be " written with the finger of God."

But we must now briefly notice a circumstance of the most deeply melancholy character. During the sojourn of Moses on the mountain the people had become restless and discontented. They did not know how to account for his long stay, and probably some of the instigators concluded that he had gone off, or that God had destroyed him. In the wickedness of their hearts they forgot all that God had done for them, and in their determined rebellion, they gathered themselves to Aaron, and demanded that he should furnish them with some other god, under whose direction they might march either back to Egypt or on to Canaan. And so ungrateful were they that they even spoke contemptuously of Moses :—" As for *this Moses*" we do not know what is become of him.

Under these circumstances, Aaron, who ought to have rebuked the people, and stood forth the champion both of God and of his brother Moses, appears to have been afraid of his people. Some have attempted to excuse him, on the plea that his life was threatened. Some say that the people killed *Hur* for opposing their wickedness; but all this is no excuse. Aaron ought to have opposed the people, to have been faithful to God, and to have left the issue in his hands. There is no reason why we should attempt to excuse the wickedness of those whose characters are written in the Scriptures. Their history is placed before us that we may learn by their example. If they had all been *perfect* characters the history itself would have been incredible, because unnatural, and therefore we are to learn the lessons intended to be taught— to be humble and fearful, and to take heed lest we fall and come into condemnation.

Some think that Aaron tried to keep the people from doing the wicked thing which they desired. He told them to bring their ornaments of gold for him to make a god of them, probably supposing that they would rather give up their determination than give up their gold; but, if this was his design, he made a great mistake—for wicked people will sacrifice any thing sooner than their evil determinations; even gold and silver will be thrown away in any quantities for the purposes of vicious indulgence. How many persons spend all their property for the poor, miserable pleasure of getting drink, and how many waste all their money upon their sensual enjoyments. There is nothing hard for the carnal heart to give up, but the love of sin. The people broke off their ear-rings and brought them to him; and when he had received the golden ornaments he melted them, and run them into a mould which he had made in the form of a calf. He chose this form, probably because he thought that it would particularly gratify the people, inasmuch as in Egypt they had been in the habit of seeing a calf worshipped; for the great Egyptian god called Osiris was worshipped under this form.

It does not appear, however, that Aaron or the people meant entirely to forsake the worship of the true God. They meant to worship the God of Israel under the similitude of a calf; for Aaron, when he had made the calf, built an altar before it, and said to the people, "To-morrow is a feast unto the LORD," or Jehovah. The sin of Aaron and the people was not their disposition utterly to forsake the worship of the true God, but to mingle with his worship that of an idol which he had forbidden. Idolatry consists not only in actually worshipping false gods instead of the true, but in making *representations*, or *images*, through which to worship the true God. The second commandment forbids every thing of the kind; and therefore to have *images* in churches or in our *houses*, and to bow down before them in any way of religious homage, is, in the sight of God, idolatry.

It is an old saying, that we are always swift enough to do evil. The Israelites rose up *early* in the morning to worship before the

L

golden calf, and after they had paid their senseless adoration, and offered sacrifices, they spent the day very much as the heathen do in the worship of their gods, viz. in gross and abominable licentiousness. But all this, just as every sin which is committed on the earth, in thought, in word, or in deed, was seen by that God whose eye nothing escapes. How must it have distressed the mind of Moses, who now for forty days and forty nights had been engaged in sweet communion with God, to hear from his mouth such language as this :—" And the Lord said unto Moses, Go, get thee down; for thy people, which thou broughtest out of the land of Egypt, have corrupted themselves: They have turned aside quickly out of the way which I commanded them: they have made them a molten calf, and have worshipped it, and have sacrificed thereunto, and said, These be thy gods, O Israel, which have brought thee up out of the land of Egypt. And the Lord said unto Moses, I have seen this people, and, behold, it is a stiff-necked people: Now therefore let me alone, that my wrath may wax hot against them, and that I may consume them: and I will make of thee a great nation." Ex. xxxiii. 7—10.

Had not Moses been a man of most extraordinary humility and self-denial, he never could have withstood the wonderful temptation of ambition which this proposal placed before him. In consequence of their sins, and especially their sin in the idolatry of the golden calf, God here offers to Moses to cut off the whole people of Israel, who had rendered themselves liable to his just indignation, and to substitute in their place the posterity of Moses: thus making him the head of a great and distinguished nation. The faith and humility of Moses prevailed against this; and his great love for the people, for whom he had already suffered so much, induced him to pray to the Lord most earnestly that he would not carry this threat into execution. He pleads with Jehovah for the sake of his own glory, and his promises to Abraham, not to cut off the people though they had so

grievously rebelled. Moses, in his earnest-
ness however, seems to have forgotten that
even if God had cut off that whole generation,
it would have been no breach of his promise
to Abraham, for if he had made a great nation
of his posterity his promise to Abraham would
have been fulfilled, for Moses was one of
the descendants of that illustrious partriarch.
But the regard which Moses here manifested
for the Divine honour, was highly pleasing in
the sight of God; and as the effectual fervent
prayer of the righteous availeth much, the
people were spared at the intercession of him
of whom they had spoken with so much disrespect, calling him *this* Moses.

When Moses had succeeded in the object
of his petition, he turned from the presence
of the Lord, and took his melancholy journey
down the mount, to attend to the unpleasant
and distressing duty arising out of this idolatry of the people. In his hands he carried
those tables of the law on which the Ten
Commandments had been written by the finger
of God. When he came to the place where
Joshua had been stationed, the people were in
the height of their boisterous merriment, and
so great was the noise of their shouting, that
it was heard far up the mount. As was natural for Joshua, who was a military man, he
supposed that the noise was that of war, and
that either there was a civil commotion in
which the people were fighting among them-

selves, or else that they had been attacked by their enemies. He said to Moses, " There is noise of war in the camp." But Moses, who knew the cause of all this noise, told him that the sound was not like that of those who shouted for victory, neither was it like the cry of those who had been beaten, but that it was the noise of *singing*, which indicated mirth. But he did not stay to converse with Joshua, he still kept on down the mountain, and when he came where he could see the transactions, he perceived that the people were dancing, and singing, and shouting before the calf. We are then told that his " anger waxed hot," and that he threw down the tables of the law, and broke them in pieces.

We stop here one moment, to correct an error which young persons are apt to fall into in relation to this action of Moses. There is nothing in the history which goes to prove that the anger of Moses was a criminal indulgence of passion. His whole conduct here was of what is called a symbolical character, and there can be no doubt that he acted under a divine impulse. His anger was no personal feeling against the people, but was intended to express his abhorrence of the crime which had been committed against God.

But Moses had a task to perform still more painful. It was to be the instrument of punishing the people for their sin. He took the golden calf, and by some method which

L 2

is not mentioned, but probably by filing, reduced it to a state of powder, and mixed it with water, which they were compelled to drink; this, no doubt, being intended to teach them that they must always expect to experience the bitter effects of their transgressions. It is most unquestionably true, as applied to all sinners, that they " shall eat the fruit of their own ways, and be filled with their own devices."

And yet Moses had a still farther duty to discharge : the rebuking of his own dear brother Aaron for the part which he had taken in this iniquitous transaction. It is remarkable that he did not ask him what apology or excuse he had to make for his concurrence with the people in the idolatry into which they had run, but he asks him in what the people had offended him, which could have induced him to revenge himself by leading his brethren into such great wickedness. This most emphatically declares the judgment which Moses entertained of the conduct of Aaron, and sets at rest all the efforts which have been made to excuse it. " Indeed," says one, " no wise man ever made a more unmeaning and foolish excuse than Aaron did. ' And Aaron said, Let not the anger of my lord wax hot: thou knowest the people, that they are set on mischief. For they said unto me, Make us gods, which shall go before us : for as for this Moses, the man that brought us up out of the land of Egypt, we wot not what is become of him. And I said unto them, Whosoever hath any gold, let them break it off. So they gave it me: then I cast it into the fire, and there came out this calf.' " Ex. xxxii. 22—24.

If the people were bent upon mischief, Aaron, the saint and servant of the Lord, who was intrusted with authority over Israel, should have ventured and suffered all extremities in opposing their mad design. But while he was as pliant as they could wish, and very active in the business, he charged all the blame on others, and spoke as if the golden calf had been produced by acci-dent, with little or no agency of his. And, besides this, he seemed to care more lest Moses should be angry, than he did for the anger of God. It was no wonder that " the Lord was angry with him to have destroyed him," as Moses tells us, in Deut. ix. 20. But Moses prayed for him also, and we have every reason to believe that he was ever after ashamed of his conduct on this occasion.

This act of idolatry, however, could not be passed over by a righteous God, who will not suffer his glory to be given to another without some dreadful manifestation of his indignation: consequently about three thousand of the people, no doubt those who had been most actively engaged, fell that day by the command of the Lord. The next day Moses brought the sin of the people to their minds; but told them that he would seek some atonement to be made. With this view he appeared before the Lord, but no atonement was directed to be made. Moses prayed with the utmost importunity, and even expressed his willingness that the Lord should cut him off and deprive him of all the promised privileges, if he would but spare the people. Here was an evidence of uncommon disinterestedness. It was as much as if he had said, " O Lord, instead of destroying Israel as a sacrifice to thy justice, and making of me a great nation, let me be the sacrifice, and spare them. And if it may not consist with thy glory to spare them otherwise, and my death may suffice for that purpose, exclude me from Canaan, and take me out of life, in any way that thou seest good: only let the people be spared." In this transaction Moses appears to be a wonderful and striking type of our Lord and Saviour Jesus Christ, who did actually lay down his life that poor sinners might be saved. How beautifully is the love of Christ displayed in the epistle to the Romans :—Therefore, being justified by faith, we have peace with God, through our Lord Jesus Christ: By whom also we have access by faith into this grace wherein we stand, and rejoice in hope of the glory of God. And not only so, but we glory in tribulations also : knowing that tribulation worketh patience ; and patience, experience; and experience, hope: and hope maketh not ashamed; because the love of God is shed abroad in our hearts by the Holy Ghost, which is given unto us. For when we were yet without strength, in due time Christ died for the ungodly. For scarcely for a righteous man will one die: yet peradventure for a good man some would even dare to die. But God commendeth his love toward us, in that, while we were yet sinners, Christ died for us. Much more then, being now justified by his blood, we shall be saved from wrath through him. For if, when we were enemies, we were reconciled to God by the death of his Son, much more, being reconciled, we shall be saved by his life. Rom. v. 1—10.

God, however, would not listen to the proposal of Moses. He directed him to go on in leading the people towards Canaan, and promises him his guiding care; but he tells him distinctly that this sin of the people of Israel, in worshipping the golden calf, should not be forgotten. "Nevertheless," says God, "in the day when I visit I will visit their sin upon them." To this very day the Jews have a saying very common among them, and just as true as it is common, "that all the calamities which have ever since befallen the nation, have, in them, a measure of the Lord's indignation for the sin of the golden calf." How true is it, that God is a "jealous God,

and will not give his glory to another."
How true, that " sin shall not go unpunished."

———

CHAPTER XV.

Moses desirous to behold the glory of God.—
Is afterwards directed to prepare two ta-
bles of stone.—Ascends the mountain
again.—Continues, as before, forty days
and nights.—Returns with the tables of
the law.—His face has a singularly bright
appearance.

In the history of Moses, we find many instances in which his faithful and persevering
prayers were answered. He had prevailed
so far as to stay the execution of the sentence
against the Israelites in the matter of the golden calf; but seems to be somewhat discouraged when God declined to be, as heretofore,
the leader of the people. Moses was told to
go and direct the people in their march to
Canaan, but God said to him, that instead of
going before them as he had heretofore done,
he would send an angel, under whose guidance
they might reach the land. When this was
told the people they mourned, and humbled
themselves before God. As the peculiar pre-

sence of God was removed from them, most
probably by the departure of the cloudy pillar,
Moses himself, no doubt acting by divine
impulse, removed the tabernacle where he
had administered the affairs of the people,
beyond the boundaries of the encampment.
This itself must have conveyed to the minds
of the people a very powerful idea of the
heavy displeasure of God : for henceforth they
would understand that he would not dwell
in the midst of them. This action of Moses
was observed by the people with great apparent interest. No sooner had he entered into
the tent, than the cloudy pillar, which in all
probability had been withdrawn since the idolatry of the golden calf, now descended again,
and stood at its door. This re-appearance of
the cloudy pillar, not over the camp, but at a
distance, and where Moses was, served to
convince the people that he had acted under
divine direction, and they seem to have been
so deeply impressed by it, that they fell down
in solemn worship. While the people were
in this situation, the sacred history tells us,
that the Lord talked with Moses, and the very
remarkable expression is used, that he "spake
unto Moses, face to face, as a man speaketh
to his friend ;" not that there was any appearance like a human form, for we are told
repeatedly that no manner of similitude of
God has ever been seen, but that there was a
voice coming out of the cloud and conversing,

very probably like what is recorded of our Saviour, in Matthew xvii. 5 :—" While he yet spake, behold, a bright cloud overshadowed them : and, behold, a voice out of the cloud, which said, This is my beloved Son, in whom I am well pleased ; hear ye him."·

Moses here pleads with God that he would not forsake the people, but that he would still lead them to Canaan; and God, in infinite mercy and condescension, granted this request also ; and tells his faithful servant that His " presence should go with them," on account of the favour which he bore to him. How honoured was Moses : truly there were none like him.

Encouraged and made bold by the success with which he had met, Moses ventured to ask of God, as a very special favour, and one which would particularly animate his soul, that God would show him his " glory." As Moses had already seen many great manifestations of the glory of God, we are here to understand by this request, something far beyond any appearance which had hitherto been made : something more spiritual in its nature. On this occasion God said to Moses, that his request, as to its full intention, could not be granted; for that if he showed his glory it would be sufficient to strike him dead, by its transcendent splendour and brightness. But he was told, that as far as a mortal could endure the sight he should be gratified. Then

God told him to stand upon a rock, and that
he would permit his glory to pass by the
place ; but that while it was passing, he would
put him in a cleft of the rock, and there cover
him with his hand, so that when the amazing
splendour of his presence was passed he might
see something which was less glorious than
God's unveiled face.   It is impossible to com-
prehend the nature of this appearance, and it
is difficult to understand the peculiar meaning
of this singular transaction.   One of the most
judicious writers on the Scriptures has said,
" The transaction was doubtless emblematic.
We can in this world only see the glory of God
as reflected from his works, or as revealed in
his word ; for the more direct display of his
essential glory is reserved for heaven.   The
rock on which Moses stood, and in the cleft of
which he was sheltered, was doubtless an em-
blem of Christ, in whose person, character, and
salvation alone, we sinners may, by faith, see
the glory of God and live : for there it appears
in softened splendour, as the sun when his
brightness is diminished by a mist is beheld
more distinctly by the human eye."
After God had so far granted the prayer of
Moses, as to promise that he should thus see
some modified exhibition of his glory, he directed him to hew two tables of stone, similar
to those which had been broken, and to take
them up into the mountain the next day,
when he would write on them, a second time,

M

the Ten Commandments. Moses did as he was commanded, and took the tables with him as he went up into the mountain. At this time God fulfilled the promise relative to his glory. And this is the circumstance as it is told in the sacred history :—" And the Lord descended in the cloud, and stood with him there, and proclaimed the name of the Lord. And the Lord passed by before him, and proclaimed, The Lord, the Lord God, merciful and gracious, long-suffering, and abundant in goodness and truth, keeping mercy for thousands, forgiving iniquity and transgression and sin, and that will by no means clear the guilty; visiting the iniquity of the fathers upon the children, and upon the children's children, unto the third and to the fourth generation." Ex. xxxiv. 5—7.

This display of the glory of God produced its proper effect upon the mind and heart of Moses. He bowed his head and worshipped; and then seized the opportunity of repeating his petition, that God would still bless the people by leading them to Canaan. This petition was granted; and then the Lord gave him further directions as to his course of conduct in the government of Israel, and prescribed certain religious institutions, which were to be strictly attended to. These things Moses was directed to write, and the whole transaction was considered as the renewal of the covenant which had been broken. As he had done before, Moses continued on the mount forty days and forty nights, miraculously sustained without food or drink.

When these forty days and nights were ended, Moses went once more down from the mount with the tables of the law in his hand;

and here we have recorded another emblematic circumstance which is remarkably curious and instructive. It was found that on the descent of Moses from the mount, the " skin of his face shone;" that is, there was a peculiar brightness about it which made it difficult to look upon. We know, that if we attempt to look at the sun when he shines out in brightness, our eyes would be so dazzled that we could not bear it, and so it is very difficult to look on any very white or bright object from which the rays of the sun are reflected. When the sun shines long on any object it imparts a brightness which does not belong to the object itself; so, in this case, Moses had been so long engaged in the contemplation of the Divine glory, that this glory was miraculously represented to the people by the extreme brightness of his face. His countenance did not shine when he came down the first time from the mount; but the reason of this is evident—he had not been then blessed with such bright displays of the glory of God, but during his second sojourn he had received large and clear discoveries of the glorious perfections of the divine character; and thus the Lord put additional honour upon him before all the people. So bright and glorious was the appearance of his face, that even Aaron was afraid to approach him, as if he had been some supernatural being. When Moses understood the cause of their fear, he put a veil upon his face whenever he conversed with the people, but he took it off when he went into the tabernacle to commune with God.

It would not be just to the subject to pass it over entirely without any remarks on its typical import, but we must of necessity be brief. By some of the most judicious writers, it was considered, 1st, that the veil on the face of Moses typified *the darkness of the law compared with the noon-tide brightness of the gospel.* " But if the ministration of death written and engraven in stones, was glorious, so that the children of Israel could not steadfastly behold the face of Moses, for the glory of his countenance ; which glory was to be done away ; how shall not the ministration of the Spirit be rather glorious ? For if the ministration of condemnation be glory, much more doth the ministration of righteousness exceed in glory. For even that which was made glorious had no glory in this respect, by reason of the glory that excelleth. For if that which is done away was glorious, much more that which remaineth is glorious. Seeing then that we have such hope, we use great plainness of speech : And not as Moses, which put a veil over his face, that the children of Israel could not steadfastly look to the end of that which is abolished : But their minds were blinded : for until this day remaineth the same veil untaken away in the reading of the Old Testament ; which veil is done away in Christ. But even unto this day, when Moses is read, the veil is upon their heart. Nevertheless, when it shall turn to the Lord, the veil shall be taken away. Now the Lord is that spirit : and where the Spirit of the Lord is, there is liberty. But we all, with open face beholding as in a glass the glory of the Lord, are changed into the same image from glory to glory, even as by the Spirit of the Lord." 2 Cor. iii. 7.—18.

The veil on the face of Moses, 2dly, typified, *the ignorance of the Jews in relation to the spiritual character of their own law.* But as it is of much less importance that we should remark upon the case as it confines itself to the Jews, than as it may be made to serve a practical purpose for ourselves, we have to say that the *veil of unbelief* is not confined to the Jewish people. The *natural,* or *unconverted* man, whether he is a Jew or a Gentile, " discerneth not the things of the spirit of God." Multitudes go to church, and hear and read the truth of God, and thousands of Sunday-school scholars also hear and read of God's salvation, and yet see no beauty in the Saviour which can induce them to accept him. The *veil* cannot be taken off, until our hearts turn to the Lord, and until we resign ourselves, in utter want of any other hope, to accept and embrace the great redemption as a pure gift from heaven. Oh, let us examine whether it can be said of us, " Ye were once *darkness,* but now are ye *light* in the Lord." Let us hear individually the voice which cries to those who are dead in trespasses and sins, " Awake, thou that sleepest, and arise from the dead, and Christ shall give thee light." If we are still in darkness, let us lift up our voice in prayer for light and faith. " Lord we believe, help thou our unbelief." Let us implore that " the eyes of our understanding may be enlightened."

When the veil is taken off, the heart is sanctified; and we become new creatures in Christ Jesus.

There is another remarkable circumstance connected with this transaction. When Moses went into the tabernacle, the veil was taken off, and he conversed with the Most High " face to face, as a man talketh with his friend." It has been universally admitted, that the tabernacle was a type of heaven. What, then, will be the blessed state of those who shall be admitted into the paradise above? Even now, amidst all the brightness of the gospel dispensation, " we see through a glass darkly;" but if we shall be so happy as to worship in the temple above, we shall see, " face to face." " Now we know only in part, but then shall we know even as we are known;" for no cloud will hide the view of the Almighty from the eyes of the redeemed and glorified. Moses was made honourable in the sight of the children of Israel, by being permitted to converse with Jehovah upon Sinai; but what shall be the glory of those who are prepared to dwell with God for ever! Let us repent and believe the gospel; let us submit our hearts to Jesus the Saviour, and then will he bring us, when time shall be no longer, to spend an eternity with him, where there shall be nothing to hide from us the full glories of his eternal presence.

CHAPTER XVI.

The building of the tabernacle, and its con-
secration.—God takes possession of it as
his dwelling-place.—Moses receives the
laws relating to the offerings.—He is com-
manded to consecrate Aaron and his sons
to the priesthood.—Transgression and pu-
nishment of Nadab and Abihu, and others.
—A variety of laws given.—Shelomith's
sin, stoned for blasphemy.

THE period in the history of Moses to
which we have now reached, was probably
the most active and busy term of his life, and
yet one about which we can have least to say.
We mean the period in which he was engaged
in superintending the building of the tabernacle. This was a task which God had
assigned to him when he was in the mount,
and there he received his orders as to the
most minute circumstances connected with
the building. God left nothing to human
skill or contrivance in the plan of this tabernacle; and there can be no doubt that this
was intended to typify, the *perfection* of all
God's plans, and his determination that no
human being should have any thing to boast

of; like the work of redemption which is all of God, so that no flesh should glory in his presence.

But, before the tabernacle could be built, materials were to be provided, and these materials are specified. An enumeration of the articles is all that we can give :—gold and silver and brass ; blue, scarlet, purple, and fine linen ; goat's hair, ram's skins dyed red, badgers' skins, and a beautiful and durable wood then called Shittim wood, but now Acacia ; and oil and spices, for the preparation of sweet incense or perfume. Besides these there were to be onyx stones, and every variety of precious stones, for the purpose of adorning the vestments of the high priest. These things were brought in abundance by the people : the gold was supplied from their bracelets and earrings, or various ornaments ; and, in truth, all the articles which were needed were poured into the treasury of the Lord in the most willing profusion. These rich ornaments, &c., the people had received from the Egyptians when they were " thrust out" in haste ; and though they had, in their wickedness, wasted some of them in their desire to have the golden calf, yet now, as a testimony of their repentance for that sin, and their disposition to obey God, they dedicated all the rest to his service. Indeed, so much was brought, that at length the workmen had to tell Moses there was much more than enough, and Moses was obliged to restrain the people in their donations.

How different from the conduct of Christians in the present day : with what reluctance do they give to the cause of the Lord, and comparatively how little. God's cause in the world is to be advanced by the labours and sacrifices of his people, and yet his people do not seem to understand their duty nor their privilege. There is no single individual who calls himself a follower of the Lord Jesus Christ, who does not owe *every thing* to God, and when God's cause needs a free and generous contribution, he is ungrateful to God if he does not go to the full extent of his means to advance it.

In this business of the building of the tabernacle, every one of the Israelites was engaged. Those who had no gold or silver or other articles, gave their personal labour ; and we are told that those women, whose hearts were interested, contributed their proportion by spinning the goats' hair and the wool, and by the weaving and the sewing that were necessary. In the work of God none can innocently be idle. Those who have no money can use their influence with others ; and those who have neither money nor influence can use the labour of their hands, and add the great assistance of their faithful prayers. No Christian can or will be idle or unfruitful if he would be safe ; for true love to God implies love for the souls of others, and there can be no love for the souls of others where there is no labour, no sacrifices, no prayers in their behalf.

The persons whom Moses employed as the head workmen, were pointed out to him by God himself, and they were, by the influence of the Holy Spirit, qualified to perform the work which was assigned them. The names of these men were *Bezaleel*, of the tribe of Judah, and *Aholiab*, of the tribe of Dan. Under them there was an immense number of inferior workmen employed; but the whole of them derived a peculiar wisdom for their work from God himself, for we are told that Moses not only called Bezaleel and Aholiab, but " *every* wise hearted man, in whose heart the *Lord had put wisdom.*" The articles contributed by the people for the work were put into the hands of these men, and they went faithfully and zealously to work; and in due time every thing was made without the least variation from the pattern or model which God had shown Moses in the mount. When the whole work was finished, and reviewed by Moses, he pronounced that all had been done agreeably to the will of God, and gave to all the workmen his solemn benediction.

In the service of God no delays are to be made. No sooner was the work for the tabernacle done, than Moses proceeded to set it up. He had led the people of Israel out of Egypt on the fifteenth day of the first month of their year. On the fiftieth day after that event the law was solemnly given. Moses then spent at least eighty days upon the mount, so, upon the lowest calculation, six months must have passed away before the work of the tabernacle was begun. It was set up on the first day of the first month of the second year; it consequently leaves just about six months as the time in which the workmen were engaged in the preparation. During this time we hear of no murmurings, no discontents, which may teach us this valuable lesson, that there is nothing better calculated to keep us from discontent and sin, than to be zealously and steadily engaged in the work of God.

No sooner was the tabernacle set up, than Moses, by solemn acts of worship, dedicated or consecrated it to the service and worship of God. He put the ark of the testimony, and the mercy seat, in their place between the cherubims; he put the table of shew-bread in its appropriate position, and placed the loaves of bread upon it; he put the golden candle-stick where he had been directed, and lighted the lamps which filled its branches; he placed the golden altar in its situation, and offered sweet incense: he planted the altar of burnt offering, and offered sacrifices upon it. Indeed he left nothing undone which had been commanded; and he had the exalted satisfaction of finishing the work with the perfect approbation of his God.

When Moses had made this solemn dedication of the house, God was pleased to accept the offering, and to take the tabernacle as his own peculiar dwelling-place among the people :—" Then a cloud covered the tent of the congregation, and the glory of the Lord filled the tabernacle. And Moses was not able to enter into the tent of the congregation, because the cloud abode thereon, and the glory of the Lord filled the tabernacle." Ex. xl. 34, 35.

We now find a great change in the manner of God's communication with Moses. Instead of calling him up to the mount he called him into the tabernacle to receive his orders. Almost the whole of the book of Leviticus is taken up in the detail of those laws which related to the worship and service, which, by way of distinction, are called the *ecclesiastical* laws, or laws which related to the Jewish people, as composing the church of God. In our history it would be out of place to go into a consideration of these laws; and with a brief remark, that God chose Aaron to be the high priest, and established the priesthood in his family, we pass on to consider a very grievous act of rebellion against God, which grew out of the ambition and irreverence of the two eldest sons of Aaron, Nadab, and Abihu.

These two young men, for reasons which

N

the sacred history does not distinctly explain, but which we are compelled to think arose out of a state nearly allied to *intoxication*, were guilty of a most grievous sin against the Lord. We ought not to charge them with intoxication, without at least having some tolerable ground on which to build this opinion, but we think that a law which God made *immediately following* their punishment, shows in some degree what their crime was. God said to Aaron, " Do not *drink wine nor strong drink*, thou, nor thy sons with thee, when ye go into the tabernacle of the congregation, lest ye die : it shall be a statute for ever throughout your generations." Levit. x. 9.

It is more than likely, that at the conclusion of the solemn dedication of the tabernacle, the whole people had feasted in token of their joy, and that Nadab and Abihu, having improperly indulged themselves, were somewhat overcome by wine. This is the only way in which their strange and sinful conduct can be accounted for ; and it teaches us one very important lesson, that there is no sin into which we may not be led, if we once depart from the strictest principles of *temperance*. The very least excitement of the system by the stimulus of liquor, at once destroys the judgment, and leads to all that is disgraceful and ruinous.

But what was the sin which Nadab and Abihu committed ? We are told in the history, that they each of them took a censer, and put fire therein, and offered strange fire before the Lord. Now, to understand their sin, we must know that *censers* were vessels generally of brass, having holes at the bottom for the purpose of admitting air, that in these censers fire was first put, then *incense* on the fire, which was burned in the presence of God. The fire which was to be used on these occasions, was that taken from the great altar of burnt offerings, which fire God himself had sent down from heaven. Now Nadab and Abihu, acting without any orders from their father, Aaron, who was the high priest, and had the sole right to give directions, took their censers, and without any consultation put ordinary fire into them, and in this way went and burned incense before the Lord. This presumptuous sin awakened at once the just indignation of the Lord, and he sent out fire from his presence and consumed them in a moment. All this appears to have been done so suddenly, that neither Moses nor Aaron had time to interfere. Had these rash young men taken one moment to consider what they were about, or had they consulted their father, Aaron, all the evil might have been avoided, but they were excited, and impatient, and headstrong, and thus met the reward of all such dispositions, by experiencing that " the wages of sin is death." Let their dreadful fate be a warning to every

young reader never to sin against the Lord—
rashness, and inconsideration, and even intemperance, will never excuse them, but he
who sins must be punished, for this is God's
declaration.

There was one individual in whose heart
this dreadful scene must have produced the
most distressing feelings, Aaron, the father of
the two unhappy and wicked young men.
It is very painful to the heart of a parent to
have a child or children cut off in the ordinary
course of nature, but how much more distressing to have them suddenly cut off, and in the
very act of transgressing against God.   We
here have reason to admire the resignation of
Aaron.   The punishment which God had
inflicted on his sons was terrible, but just;
and the sacred history tells us, " Aaron held
his peace :" he made no complaints.   It was
the Lord's will, and he had nothing to say
against it.   Let every reader repent and turn
to God, and then death will never overtake
him unawares, or in a state of rebellion.

After this dreadful transaction, Moses received from God many additional laws relating
to the arrangements of the people, but none
which it is necessary to mention in this history, further than to name some of the most
prominent, which were, laws relating to the
kinds of food the people were permitted to
eat; laws concerning the disease called leprosy; laws as to the great day of atonement

and its various services ; laws relating to marriage ; laws concerning various feasts both annual and occasional ; and a repetition of the laws concerning idolatry.

Before we conclude this chapter, however, we ought to mention another very striking instance of the anger of God against sin. The story is short, but full of valuable instruction.

It appears that while they were in Egypt, a woman by the name of Shelomith, belonging to the tribe of Dan, had married an Egyptian, and their son had, with the mixed multitude, followed the Israelites when they left the land of Egypt. Some dispute arose between this man and one of the Israelites, and they appear to have tried to end their dispute by a battle, as many wicked persons have done since their time. As one sin most generally paves the way for another, this son of Shelomith blasphemed the name of the Lord : he swore, and thus took the name of the Lord in vain—a sin of the most awful and aggravated character. Those who heard him, brought him at once to Moses, and Moses, as there had no law yet been made, defining or fixing the punishment which was due to blasphemy, ordered him to be put under guard until he could inquire the will of the Lord in the matter. When he did this, God directed that the·blasphemer should be taken without the boundaries of the camp, and that all who had heard the blasphemy

2 N

should lay their hands on the head of the man, in token that their testimony was true, and as signifying that his sin was upon his own head. When this was done he was to be stoned to death. This crime was the occasion of the following law, which was ever afterwards in force among the Jews as long as they continued a- nation. "And he that blasphemeth the name of the Lord, he shall surely be put to death, and all the congregation shall certainly stone him : as well the stranger, as he that is born in the land, when he blasphemeth the name of the Lord, shall he be put to death." Levit. xxiv. 16. According to the command of God this wicked son of Shelomith was stoned to death, as the just punishment of his blasphemy.

How many there are who are in the habit of using the name of God in profane swearing. This is blasphemy, and will be most dreadfully visited. What enmity against God must be in the heart of an individual, when curses and blasphemies against God proceed out of his mouth. And if he who despised Moses' law died without mercy under two or three witnesses, of what punishment shall they be thought worthy or deserving who despise and abuse the gospel of the Son of God? Let us, then, learn to avoid all anger and fighting, and to reverence the holy name of God : knowing that not only liars, and drunkards, and thieves, and murderers, but

that also *all swearers* shall have their portion
in that lake which burneth for ever.

CHAPTER XVII.

*Moses, at the command of God, numbers the
people.—Directed as to the method of their
encampment.—Leaves the wilderness of
Sinai.—Hobal.—The people complain.—
Moses' faith is staggered.—Quails sent in
anger.—Transgression of Miriam and
Aaron.*

ABOUT one month after the setting up of
the tabernacle, God ordered Moses to enter
upon the task of numbering the people, and
appointed one principal person out of each
tribe to assist him. This numbering embraced
only those who were twenty years old and
upward; the women and children, and probably very old men, together with the mixed
multitude, were omitted. The purpose of
their being numbered is generally supposed
to have been to prove that the word of God
was true in relation to the great increase of
the seed of Jacob, and also to prepare the
way for their regular march and encampments,
as they were soon to depart from Sinai. The

number amounted to six hundred and three thousand, five hundred and fifty-five effective men.

As God intended that the people should speedily remove from Sinai, he directed the order in which they should march and encamp. They were to encamp in four grand divisions, having the tabernacle in the centre. " The tribe of Judah, from which Christ sprang, took the highest station, and under it were ranked the tribes of Issachar and Zebulun, the younger brothers of Judah by the same mother. The tribe of Reuben was appointed to lead the second division, and under it the tribes of Simeon and Gad. The three tribes descended from Rachel formed the third division; and the remaining three tribes the fourth division. There was a little variation when they marched. When the people were encamped, one division of the people was placed on each quarter over against the tabernacle; but when they marched, two divisions went before and two behind it.

After some additional laws and regulations had been made, which are found recorded in the first nine chapters of the book of Numbers, God gave the signal for the marching of the people. This event occurred on the twentieth day of the second month of the second year of their departure from Egypt. They had now been very nearly one year encamped in the wilderness of Sinai, where they had seen the most wonderful displays of the power and glory of God, and where every thing had been arranged relating to their future prosperity, both as a people and a church. They had no doubt received intimations to be in readiness to march, and then, on the day before spoken of, God gave the signal, by the rising up of the cloud, which had hitherto rested on the tabernacle; and they commenced their journey in the order previously appointed. It will, of course, be impossible for us to enter into all the minute circumstances connected with their journeyings, but we hope to omit no important matter which serves in any way to illustrate the character of Moses.

Previous, however, to their departure from Sinai, a very interesting scene took place between Moses and his relation Hobab. As they were about to go to the land of Canaan, Moses appears to have been particularly anxious that Hobab should go with them, and he uses the most tender and touching language of invitation:—" We are journeying," says he, " to the place of which the Lord said unto us, I will give it you. Come thou with us, and we will do thee good, for the Lord hath spoken good concerning Israel." Hobab appears to have received this kind offer rather uncourteously, and says, " I will not go, but I will depart to mine own country and my kindred." Moses was not discouraged by this repulse, and says to him, still more ur-

gently, " leave us not I pray thee ;" and then
to give an additional weight to his entreaty,
he tells Hobab how useful he might be to
them by his knowledge of the wilderness.
We are inclined to think that the importunity
of Moses at length prevailed ; for we find that
the posterity of Hobab had a possession assigned to them in the land of Canaan.

The conduct of Moses on this occasion is
a lovely instance of the tender concern which
he had for the welfare of his friends ; and it
ought to teach all those who love the Lord,
how much might be accomplished if they
would only wisely and tenderly press the
claims of religion on their relatives and friends.
How can we be content, that those whom we
love should remain in their sins, while we
leave any thing undone to draw them to
religion ?   Let us urge and entreat them : let
us show them by our own temper and conduct
the influence of divine truth, and let us pray
for them without ceasing.   How happy will
it make us, if our friends and their families,
through our instrumentality, find a possession
in the heavenly Canaan.   This may be done
if we are faithful.

From this happy and interesting circumstance we turn to one of a most melancholy
description.   For some reasons not mentioned
in the history, we are told that the people
murmured against the Lord ; and again they
were severely punished.   But hardly had the

punishment ceased before there was another dissatisfaction, on account of their not having flesh to eat. They expressed themselves tired of being compelled to eat the *manna ;* and with a spirit of undutiful ingratitude, contrasted the food which they had enjoyed in Egypt with the food which God had so miraculously and bountifully given them. They chose to forget, that though they ate fish from the river Nile, and had plenty of vegetables and fruit, they were all the time in a state of dreadful slavery, and subject to the hardest work, and the most excessive cruelty ; even to having their children taken from them and murdered. But so it is ; when our desires are not at once gratified, we are apt to overvalue *former* blessings, and undervalue *present* mercies. In every way which could be imagined, the situation of the Israelites was far superior to what it had been in Egypt—they had God for their leader and protector, and had enough to eat and drink. But nothing would satisfy but *meat ;* and because their *desire,* or *lust* as the history calls it, was not satisfied, they complain against the Lord.

It is here that we have the *first* instance in which the *faith* of Moses seemed to fail : he was not only displeased with the people, but he addressed himself to God in a discontented spirit, and without reflecting by whose power he acted, and under whose protection he was, he asks, in a tone of irritation, " Whence

should *I* have flesh to give unto all this people;" and even begged that he might die.
This cannot be excused. God had never expected *him* to supply the people with food;
and what right had he to wish to relinquish
the situation in which God had placed him?
But the Lord had a work to do by Moses,
and he did not immediately punish this failure
of his confidence, and this improper indulgence
of a complaining disposition. He appointed
seventy men of the elders of the congregation
to assist him in the discharge of his arduous
duties, and promised to gratify the wishes of
the people. Yes, God promised to gratify
the wishes of the people; but this very gratification was intended as their punishment.
How little do we know what is for our best
interest, and there can be no doubt that the
very granting of our requests for temporal
mercies, if they are made in a spirit of discontent with what we already have, would do us
incalculable injury.

How many examples do we see of this.
A man in moderate circumstances becomes
unhappy in his situation, and desires to be
rich and increased with goods. By and by
he becomes rich; and what does he find?
that his happiness is increased? No: he finds
that with his increasing riches he has increasing troubles and increasing cares; and that
what he had supposed would be for his happiness turns out for his misery. There could

no greater evil happen to any man, than that God should grant him his foolish desires. It is among the mercies of God to those who love him, that he withholds from them whatever would be hurtful, for we are so short-sighted that we never know what would advance our greatest good. Let us love God, and serve him, and then we are sure that nothing can happen but for our advantage; for it is the declaration of the word of God, that "all things work together for good to those who love God;" and even the very afflictions of life are among the blessings which true believers experience at the hand of God; for he says, our light afflictions which are but for a moment, work out for us a far more exceeding and eternal weight of glory, while we look not at the things which are seen, but at the things which are not seen; that is spiritual and heavenly things.

But to return to the history. God sent upon the people of Israel *quails*, in such abundance, that they lay scattered for twenty miles round the camp in every direction, and to the depth of two cubits; and so eager were the people, that they spent two days in collecting them. They then spread them about to dry, so that they might keep the longer. The whole conduct of the people shows that they were resolved on the indulgence of their appetites; and just like all persons who give way to improper indulgence, either in eating or

O

drinking, they suffered for it dreadfully. No sooner had they begun to eat the quails, which they did, with a voracious appetite, than the anger of God fell upon them. We are told that he brought upon them a great plague; but what that plague was we are not told. Whatever it was, there was an immense destruction among the people, so much so that the place where they buried those who died of that plague was called *Kibroth hattavah*, which means the *graves of lust*. And thus what they desired, and what they murmured after, when it was given proved the occasion of their destruction. Let us learn, that God can punish as well by plenty as by scarcity; and it will often happen that those things after which men have lusted, become their torment and their death. Whence come most of the diseases to which we are subject? Come they not even of luxury and debauchery, and *intemperance* in eating and drinking? Indeed, if we except a few cases, every grave is a grave of lust, and there might be, as an incription, put up over the gate of every burying-ground—Kibroth Hattavah.

About this time a very singular circumstance took place, which shows the noble and disinterested spirit of Moses. Among the seventy elders whom God had appointed to assist Moses, there were two, named Eldad and Medad, who being particularly influenced by the spirit of God so to do, began to prophecy, or, as it here means, to preach in the camp; no doubt calling the people to repent of their sins, and turn from their rebellions. Some young man, whose name is not mentioned, ran and told Moses what these men were doing, and Joshua, who was present when the information was given, advised that they should be stopped or silenced. He was, no doubt, influenced by an earnest zeal for the honour of Moses; and was under the impression, that if these men were permitted to go on, they might gain an influence with the people which might be turned to the disadvantage of Moses. But Moses thought far otherwise. His only object was to seek the glory of God, and he told Joshua not to be alarmed on his account, for that he wished all the people of the Lord were prophets: holy and devoted to God. The true people of God are every one of them, in a certain sense, prophets or preachers of the gospel; for though they do not go into pulpits, as those who are public ministers, and there preach the unsearchable riches of Christ, yet they preach Christ by their lives, according to the exhortation of our blessed Lord, " Let your light so shine before men, that they may see your good works, and glorify your Father who is in heaven."

The trait in the character of Moses, or that disposition of his mind which was manifested in this transaction, was a noble disinterestedness. He did not care any thing about his own popularity so long as the glory of God could be advanced. He appears much like John the Baptist, who said, in reference to Christ, " *He* must increase, but *I* must decrease."

But the next circumstance which is mentioned in the history, is one which perhaps was the most painful which ever occurred to Moses in his private capacity. Often, very often, had he been cut to the heart by the ingratitude and rebellion of the people, because the honour of God was concerned; but here we have a difficulty of a family nature; a kind of domestic quarrel, in which his dear brother Aaron and his sister Miriam were the aggressors, and his wife the subject. We do not know all the circumstances of the case: all we know is, that Aaron and Miriam spake against Moses in relation to Zipporah, his wife. What the ground of objection was we are not informed, and it would be vain to conjecture. But nothing could excuse the rebellion and unkindness of Miriam and Aaron on this occasion.

When persons are heated with anger, they seldom confine themselves to the subject of the original quarrel, but go on, from subject to subject, till they have vented all their ill humour. It appears that Miriam and Aaron, not content with quarreling with Moses about his wife, insinuated that he took too much

upon himself, as the Lord had spoken to the
people by them as well as by him.

To this charge Moses answered nothing.
The sacred history tells us that he was the
meekest man on the earth, and every one who
is at all acquainted with his life, knows that this
was the case from the many instances which
are recorded in which it was exhibited. But
though on the present occasion Moses was
entirely silent, and left his cause in the hands
of God, he was fully vindicated. God suddenly spoke to him, and ordered that he, and
Aaron, and Miriam, should go to the door of
the tabernacle. When there, God told them
that it was his pleasure thus particularly to
distinguish his servant Moses; and he asks
why they were not afraid to speak against
him. Then the anger of the Lord was kindled against them, and the cloud arose from
the tabernacle in token of the departure of
God. No sooner was this done, than Aaron
looked on Miriam, and found that God had
punished her by afflicting her with leprosy.

Astonished and alarmed he appealed to Moses, and begged that he would intercede for
them. It is here that the character of Moses appears in one of its most lovely aspects. Though
he had been deeply injured, both on his wife's
account, and by having insinuations thrown
upon himself, he forgot and forgave it all.
Without one moment's hesitation, he presented
himself before the Lord, and prayed for his

offending sister, and for his sake God forgave and healed her. What a beautiful illustration of those many exhortations of our Saviour, which enjoin the forgiveness of injuries ; and not only their forgiveness, but that we should strive, by every means in our power, to do good to those who hate us, and to pray for those who despitefully use us and persecute us. We can mention but a single case :—

" Then came Peter to him, and said, Lord how oft shall my brother sin against me, and I forgive him ? till seven times ? Jesus saith unto him, I say not unto thee, until seven times ; but, until seventy times seven. Therefore is the kingdom of heaven likened unto a certain king, which would take account of his servants. And when he had begun to reckon, one was brought unto him which owed him ten thousand talents : But forasmuch as he had not to pay, his lord commanded him to be sold, and his wife and children, and all that he had, and payment to be made. The servant therefore fell down, and worshipped him, saying, Lord, have patience with me, and I will pay thee all. Then the lord of that servant was moved with compassion, and loosed him, and forgave him the debt. But the same servant went out, and found one of his fellow-servants which owed him an hundred pence ; and he laid hands on him, and took him by the throat, saying, pay me that thou owest. And his fellow-servant fell down at his feet, and besought him, saying, have patience with me, and I will pay thee all. And he would not; but went and cast him into prison, till he should pay the debt. So when his fellow-servants saw what was done, they were very sorry, and came and told unto their lord all that was done. Then his lord, after that he had called him, said unto him, O thou wicked servant, I forgave thee all that debt, because thou desiredst me: Shouldest not thou also have had compassion on thy fellow-servant, even as I had pity on thee? And his lord was wroth, and delivered him to the tormentors, till he should pay all that was due unto him. So likewise shall my heavenly Father do also unto you, if ye from your hearts forgive not every one his brother their trespasses." Matt. xviii. 21—35.

CHAPTER XVIII.

*Spies sent to examine Canaan.—Character
of Joshua and Caleb.—The people murmur at the report of the spies.—Are excluded from Canaan, and doomed to
wander in the wilderness.—The Sabbath
breaker stoned.—Rebellion of Korah and
his company.*

At the time which our history now con-
templates, Moses had led the people to the
very border of the land of Canaan, and had
not something here occurred which provoked
the Lord to anger, they might have taken
possession of the land at once. We learn
from what Moses says, in the first chapter of
Deuteronomy, that the people suggested to
him the idea of sending spies to search out
the land, and he, not suspecting that it was
their unbelief which induced them to suggest
such a thing, was led to approve their proposal, and to consult the Lord on the matter.
There was evidently no kind of necessity for
sending spies to search out the land, because
as God had promised that they should possess
it, all they had to do was to put implicit confidence in Him who had never in one single

instance deceived them. God seems to have permitted this also to punish their unbelief, for the very searching of the land, instead of removing their unbelieving fears, increased them, and proved the occasion of their actual exclusion from it.

The persons who were sent as spies were pointed out by God himself to Moses. One was taken from each tribe, and such persons were taken as were distinguished among the people. There were only two of them who are particularly distinguished in the future history, *Caleb* the son of Jephunneh, of the tribe of Judah, and *Joshua* the son of Nun, belonging to the tribe of Ephraim.

As soon as these twelve men were appointed, Moses gave them their special orders. They were to commence at the southern part of the land, and go north, to the mountains, and then return through another section. They were required to ascertain what sort of people inhabited the various parts; whether they were strong or weak, and what were their numbers. They were to examine, as well as they were able, the kind and quality of the land, whether fruitful or unproductive. They were to notice whether the country was well wooded. They were to be particular in ascertaining whether the people dwelt in tents or in strong holds; that is, walled cities. And, as a final direction, Moses told them to bring back some specimen of the fruits of the land. The season was favourable for this, as it was the time of the first ripe grapes.

The spies obeyed the directions given; and on their return, when they had reached the brook called *Eshcol*, they cut down a branch with a bunch of grapes so large that two men were compelled to carry it. Thy slung it over a pole, and either carried it thus in their hands, or rested the ends of the pole on their

shoulders. They also brought figs and pomegranates. The spies were occupied in their business forty days, and they were miraculously protected by God; for it is surprising that the Canaanites did not suspect their business. At the end of the forty days, however, they returned in safety, and made their report.

It appears that ten out of the twelve spies were of a cowardly and rebellious and discontented disposition. They reported that the land was very fruitful, but they said that the people were strong, and that their cities were walled, and that they saw the gigantic descendants of Anak. Caleb and Joshua saw what was likely to be the effect produced on the people by this representation; and they endeavoured to counteract the evil which this account would naturally produce. Caleb endeavoured to encourage the people, by saying that there was no difficulty; that though their cities were walled, and the people warlike, they had God with them, and, consequently, could easily conquer. But the other ten contradicted him, and repeated their conviction that the Israelites would never be able to stand before them. Besides this, not content with exaggerating the truth, and making every thing appear as bad as they could, they descended to tell a lie, and stated that the climate was very unhealthy, and that the inhabitants were so monstrous that they themselves appeared like grasshoppers in comparison.

This evil report had the effect of setting the people to crying, just like children, when they are afraid or disappointed; and they fell again into their old sin of murmuring against

God. With a most ungrateful and rebellious spirit, they wished that they had died in Egypt, or that they had died in the wilderness; and, with the most daring impiety, charged God with having brought them out of Egypt for the very purpose of destruction. These rebellious and wicked feelings led them to declare that they would forsake God as their leader, and Moses and Aaron, and make them a captain, and then return to Egypt. Moses and Aaron fell on their faces in prayer and supplication for the people, and Joshua and Caleb tried, by every means of persuasion, to put a stop to the rebellion, but all in vain. The people even went so far as to threaten to stone these truly valuable and righteous men.

All these things brought on a crisis in their history which is of the most melancholy character. The glory of the Lord appeared, and God told Moses of his determination to punish them severely, by utterly disinheriting them. As was his custom under such circumstances Moses resorts to prayer, and so far succeeded in his petition that God did not disinherit the people, but as they had filled up the measure of their iniquity by this last and most wicked rebellion, he pronounced a sentence against them of the most severe and dreadful character. They had impiously wished that they had died in the wilderness :—" Say unto them, As truly as I live, saith the Lord, as ye have spoken in mine ears, so will I do to you: Your carcases shall fall in this wilderness; and all that were numbered of you, according to your whole number, from twenty years old and upward, which have murmured against me, doubtless ye shall not come into the land, concerning which I sware to make you dwell therein, save Caleb the son of Jephunneh, and Joshua the son of Nun." Numb. xiv. 28—30. Here we find that, in consequence of this sin, though they were now on the very borders of Canaan, every individual among them who was twenty years of age and upwards when they came out of Egypt, was doomed to die in the wilderness, and never enjoy the blessings of the land of Canaan. This was a most dreadful but just termination of their series of rebellions. Forty years more were they to wander in the wilderness till every one of that rebellious generation was dead. Oh, how terrible is the righteous judgment of God. Let us fear his displeasure, and flee to the cross of Christ for pardon and salvation.

From this sentence of exclusion from Canaan, we have seen there were two exceptions —Joshua and Caleb; and these exceptions were made because they had brought a favourable account of the land, and strove with all their might and influence to prevent the rebellion of the people. The character of Joshua we know from the whole history, for a very distinguished and faithful servant of God.

P

Of Caleb we do not know so much, because he was less conspicuous in the history, but God himself has seen fit to draw his character in the very strongest terms, when he says, " My servant, Caleb, has followed me fully." What greater evidence can be given of the excellence of his religious character : it implied, that he had faithfully discharged the duty to which he had been appointed, and was ready for any service, no matter how difficult or dangerous, if it would only advance the honour of the Lord ; that he relied implicitly on the promises of God, and went forward in the way of his duty with patience and fortitude and perseverance. What a truly fine character. Such as these shall surely inherit the blessings of the heavenly Canaan.

" And they rose up early in the morning, and gat them up into the top of the mountain, saying, Lo, we be here, and will go up unto the place which the Lord hath promised : for we have sinned. And Moses said, Wherefore now do ye transgress the commandment of the Lord ? but it shall not prosper. Go not up, for the Lord is not among you ; that ye be not smitten before your enemies. For the Amalekites and the Canaanites are there before you, and ye shall fall by the sword : because ye are turned away from the Lord, therefore the Lord will not be with you. But they presumed to go up unto the hill-top : nevertheless the ark of the covenant of the

Lord, and Moses, departed not out of the camp. Then the Amalekites came down, and the Canaanites which dwelt in that hill, and smote them, and discomfited them, even unto Hormah." Numb. xiv. 40—45.

We must go back one moment. The very day God pronounced on the people the sentence that none of that generation should ever reach the land of Canaan, he gave them orders to turn back from the borders of the promised land towards the eastern, or what is called the Elanetic gulf of the Red Sea; and in the very wilderness through part of which they had already once passed, wander up and down as he should lead them, till, some by one kind of death, and some by another, the whole generation that came out of Egypt should be dead, and none left to inherit Canaan but those who were under twenty years of age, and the children who should be born in the meantime. The apostle Paul tells us, and the whole history of the people of Israel confirms it, that " it is a fearful thing to fall into the hands of the living God."

Agreeably to the direction of God, Moses now led the people back from the borders of Canaan; and in the wilderness they wandered from station to station for nearly thirty-eight years, of which no particular account is given us in the history. In the life of Moses, then, we have a blank of about thirty-eight years, in relation to which there are no sources of

information.   We have, in the thirty-third
chapter of the book of Numbers, the names
of the different places at which they encamped,
but how long they staid at each, or what occurred, the Scriptures do not inform us, and consequently we must be entirely silent.   There
are only two incidents which are particularly
mentioned, and one of these is intended to
convince us of the jealousy of God for the
honour of his own law.   We shall give it in
the language of Scripture, with but one or
two additional observation :—" And while
the children of Israel were in the wilderness,
they found a man that gathered sticks upon
the Sabbath day.   And they that found him
gathering sticks, brought him unto Moses and
Aaron, and unto all the congregation.   And
they put him in ward, because it was not declared what should be done to him.   And the
Lord said unto Moses, The man shall be
surely put to death : all the congregation shall
stone him with stones without the camp.
And all the congregation brought him without
the camp, and stoned him with stones, and
he died ; as the Lord commanded Moses."
Numb. xv. 32—36.

We here very distinctly perceive God's
determination that his Sabbath day was to be
kept holy ; and that no single departure could
pass unpunished.   It might be thought a very
little thing to gather a few sticks on the Sabbath day, but nothing is little which violates

a command of God. So we may think it a
small thing to take a walk for pleasure, or
make a visit of mere ceremony, or take a
journey, or to attend to our business when
very much pressed, but we forget all the
while that each of these small things dis-
honours the law of God, and is sinful in his
sight.

The only other circumstance which is mentioned in Scripture, as occurring during the
period of their thirty-eight years' wandering in
the wilderness, is the dreadful rebellion of
Korah, *Dathan*, and *Abiram*, who, with two
hundred and fifty princes of the congregation,
" gathered themselves together against Moses,
and against Aaron, and said unto them, Ye
take too much upon you, seeing all the congregation are holy, every one of them, and
the Lord is among them : wherefore then lift
ye up yourselves above the congregation of
the Lord?"   This, however, like all the other
instances of opposition to the authority of
Moses and Aaron, had a tendency to confirm
that authority; and, to add greatly to the
honour which God had put upon them. As
on similar occasions, so on this, the only de-
fence which Moses resorted to against the
evil insinuations and rebellion of these men,
was an appeal to God in prayer, humbly seek-
ing direction and assistance. When he had
done this on the present occasion, he proceeded calmly to argue with these infatuated

men; and finding that they were not willing
to listen to reason, he was obliged to tell them
that God would take the matter into his own
hand, and he predicted that Korah and his
company would be destroyed by what we call
an earthquake.   He told them that he would
rest the truth of his pretensions on this very
thing, and directed them to appear before the
Lord on the morrow, with their censers in
their hands, and let the matter be decided by
God himself, between him and Aaron on the
one side, and them on the other.   With most
daring presumption the two hundred and fifty
men came with their censers, and Korah and
Dathan and Abiram, with those whom they
influenced, stood in the door of their tents to
see the issue of this contest.   All at once the
glory of the Lord shone conspicuously, and
God told Moses to go immediately and exhort
the people to separate themselves from Korah
and his company, and the most of the congregation did so: they left these wicked men
with a few adherents, and their own families,
and silently waited to see what would be
done.   No sooner had the great mass of the
congregation separated themselves from these
men, than there was an earthquake: the
ground opened under the tents of Korah, Dathan, and Abiram, and they and all that continued with them, were swallowed up alive.
And no sooner was this done, than fire came
out from the Lord and consumed the two

hundred and fifty men that presumed, contrary
to the command of God to offer incense

It would have been supposed that so dreadful and wonderful an instance of the wrath of
God would at least have kept the people from
rebellion for a little time ; but strange as it
may appear, on the very next day, they ac-
cused Moses and Aaron of destroying those
who perished, and this again brought on
themselves the anger of God.   A plague broke
out among the people, and though Moses and
Aaron hasted to offer an atonement for the
people, before Aaron had time to get a censer,
and put fire and incense on it, no less than
fourteen thousand seven hundred of the rebels
had perished.   It is dreadful to contemplate

the rebellions of this people, and it is melancholy to think how little the judgments of God affected them. But such is the conduct of sinners in every age; mercies and judgments fail to reform them. What an awful scene will take place at the day of judgment, when all the wicked of every generation shall be cast into hell, there to suffer the vengeance of eternal fire. Oh, let us repent and flee to Jesus, who will be to us a refuge from the storm of God's most righteous indignation.

As a part of the rebellion of Korah had been in relation to the *right of Aaron and his sons* to execute the office of the priesthood, God saw fit finally to settle that matter by a miracle. He directed that Moses should take twelve rods, and write on each rod the name of the prince of the tribe to which its owner belonged, and on the rod which was for the tribe of Levi to write the name of Aaron. These rods were then to be placed in the tabernacle before the ark of the testimony, and the choice of God was to be ascertained by the rod which blossomed. All this was done, and the next day, when the rods were brought forth, it was discovered that the rod of the tribe of Levi, which had the name of Aaron upon it, not only budded and blossomed, but actually bore almonds. This decided the service of the tabernacle to be in the tribe of Levi, and the priesthood in the family of

Aaron; and we never afterwards hear of this being questioned, though the people fell into other rebellions.

———

CHAPTER XIX.

Death of Miriam.—Sin of Moses and Aaron, with their punishment.—Death of Aaron. —Moses opposed by king Arad.—Murmuring of the people, and plague of fiery serpents.—Brazen serpent.—Sihon and Og conquered.

IT was mentioned in the last chapter, that during a period of thirty-seven or thirty-eight years we have very little account of the wanderings of the Israelites, and of course that there is a corresponding blank in the history of Moses. There can be little doubt but that he spent that long period in comparative enjoyment, and that the people were much less addicted to the sins of rebellion and murmuring than they had been in the first year or eighteen months after they left the land of Egypt. During this period of thirty-seven or thirty-eight years, the sentence which God had pronounced upon the people, that they should wander in the wilderness until all those who were twenty years old and upwards, when they left the land of Egypt, had perished, was now nearly fulfilled; and they again approached the borders of the promised land. While they were encamped at a place called Kadesh, in the wilderness of Zin, (not the same places which, under nearly the same names, are mentioned before) Moses was called upon to bear an afflictive dispensation in the death of his sister Miriam, who died at the age of one hundred and thirty years, and was buried in Kadesh.

We come now to what may well be considered the most melancholy portion of our history. Shortly after the death of Miriam, we find that the water, with which the people had been supplied, completely failed. This, as they were now on the borders of the promised land, God no doubt permitted, in order to try the faith of the people; and, alas! they proved that in their hearts they were still like their fathers: they had not yet learned to put their confidence in God. They once more murmured against God, and against Moses. On this, as on all other occasions Moses thought only of resorting to God for direction, and God gave him plain and explicit commands. Those commands were to take his rod; to assemble the people; and to *speak* to the rock which was before them. Until this time, amidst all the rebellions of the people, Moses had been faithful, and had in no respect disobeyed the direct and positive commands of God. But on this occasion he did fail; and though the Scripture account of it is short, it is long enough to let us see the frailty of man, and the terrible justice of God. Instead of only *speaking* to the rock, as God had done, Moses *smote it twice:* water came out to relieve the necessities of the people, but this one act of disobedience brought on him the anger of a pure and holy God, whose commands must be obeyed. We will try to give as good an account of this melancholy affair as the brevity of the history will allow us.

It would appear that when Moses went out to obey the command of God, he was certainly under the influence of some most improper feeling towards the people. Whatever the feeling was, it produced the most disastrous results. From all that occurred, we should be afraid that by his long and quiet rule over the people, he had been a little lifted up with pride, and that as there had been very little murmuring or rebellion for nearly thirty-eight years, he became angry at the people for the disrespect which they showed him. Pride and anger lead to improper speaking. We think that all this can be discovered in the history. "Ye rebels," said he; a very improper method of address, and which shows that he was in a state of undue excitement of temper; and then, lifted up for the moment by a conceit of his own superiority, and forgetting his dependance upon God, he said, " must

WE bring you water out of this rock?" This was at once a failure to ascribe the glory to God, and is called by God himself both unbelief and irreverence; for thus spake the Lord, " Ye believed me not to sanctify me in the eyes of the children of Israel." Thus, anger, unbelief, and want of reverence, appear to have constituted the sin of Moses, for he called them rebels, and he smote the rock twice when he was not told to do it at all, and he said WE when he ought to have said GOD. For this transgression Moses was excluded from the land of Canaan; and like the rest of the generation which came out of Egypt, he, too, was to die in the wilderness; a monument of the holiness of that God who cannot look upon the least sin without the utmost abhorrence. That Moses and Aaron repented, in great bitterness of sorrow of this sin, which had thus withdrawn from them the favour of God, there can be no question, and God forgave them, and blotted out their iniquity, so that they died in peace, and in the sure and certain hope of a resurrection to eternal glory; but God did not see fit to revoke his sentence as to their exclusion from the earthly Canaan, and so, though Moses saw it from Mount Nebo, as we shall discover in the subsequent chapters, yet his feet never entered it. Oh, how terrible is even one sin. We have all reason to pray,—God be merciful to us sinners.

Moses, though he found himself excluded from Canaan, did not permit his zeal to relax in the cause of God and of his people. Between the place of their encampment and the land of Canaan, there lay the territory of the Edomites, or descendants of Esau, and Moses sent a very respectful and proper request to the king of that country to be permitted to pass through the land by the public road. The king of Edom refused his request, however, in a very uncivil manner, and prepared to resist, if Moses should attempt to pass. As the Edomites were descendants of Esau, the brother of Jacob, from whom the Israelites were descended, God would not permit Moses to force his passage through their country though he could easily have done it. He preferred that Moses should take the people by a more circuitous or round-about way, which would avoid the territory of Edom. They turned, therefore, and went into the wilderness, as near the southern border of Edom as they could keep without encroaching, and encamped at Mount Hor.

At this place Moses was called upon to suffer another great affliction in the death of his brother—he who had been his companion from the moment that he first went to Pharaoh to demand the release of the people; he who had been his friend and counsellor. It is true that on one occasion Aaron had been guilty in the matter of the golden calf, and on

Q

another that he had joined with Miriam in reproaching Moses; but with these two exceptions, and they were but momentary, they had lived in the utmost peace and harmony and affection, just as brothers ought to live. But it is the will of God that the best of friends and the most affectionate of relatives should part: they cannot always live together. Sin which brought ruin into the world brought death also, and now all must die. Happy are those friends, who when they separate on earth have the prospect of meeting in heaven, never to be separated. "Blessed are the dead who die in the Lord;" and blessed are the living who have a hope in God which maketh not ashamed.

" Friend after friend departs!
    Who hath not lost a friend?
There is no union here of hearts,
    Which hath not here an end.
Were this frail world our final rest,
Living or dying, none were blest.

" Beyond the flight of time,
    Beyond the reign of death,
There surely is some blessed clime
    Where life is not a breath;
Nor life's affections, transient fire,
Whose sparks fly upward and expire.

" There is a world above,
    Where parting is unknown,
A long eternity of Love
    Formed for the good alone ;
And Faith beholds the dying here
Translated to the glorious sphere.

" Thus, star by star declines,
  Till all are passed away ;
  As morning high and higher shines,
  To pure and perfect day,
  Nor sink those stars in empty night,
  But hide themselves in heaven's own light."

There were some circumstances about the death of Aaron which are very striking and peculiar. He, it will be recollected, was the high priest of God among the Jewish people. When God, then, informed Moses that Aaron must die before they entered into Canaan, because he had joined with him in the sin about the water from the rock, he was directed to take Aaron and Eleazar, the eldest son of Aaron, and bring them to Mount Hor. There he was to strip Aaron of his priestly garments and put them on Eleazar, in token that the office of high priest had been transferred from one to the other. Moses did this, and Aaron with the most perfect resignation to the will of God submitted to it; and, then, without pain or sickness or distress, laid himself down and died. His eyes were closed by Moses and Eleazer, who wept over him with the tenderness of a brother and a son. Much as he had of imperfection in his character, on the whole, he was in that dark age a bright example of devotedness to God—he had truly repented of his sins ; he had, by faith in the Saviour who was to come, laid hold of the promise of God, and died in peace, and now rests in glory. When Moses and Eleazar had

given vent to their feelings, they descended
from the mount, and as Aaron was no longer
with them, but the people saw Eleazar clothed
in the garments of his father, they understood
that he was dead ; and though they had often
reviled him, and rebelled against him while
living, they mourned for him when dead.
According to the custom of the times they
mourned thirty days, and the sacred history
clearly intimates that his death was universally
regretted, for " all the congregation mourned
for him, even the whole house of Israel."

When the thirty days were ended, during
which the people had mourned for Aaron,
their journey was resumed, and they were
opposed on their march by one of the petty
kings of the land, called Arad, but he was
soon defeated, and there was but little inter-
ruption to the journey on his account.   There
was one circumstance, however, which greatly
distressed the people, viz. that they were
compelled to go round the land of Eden by a
long and troublesome march, and we are told
that the " soul of the people was much discouraged because of the way ;" that is, they
were very much out of spirits, and disappointed
because they could not get immediately to
Canaan. As usual with them, this led to
murmuring against God and against Moses,
and they took up the old complaint that they
were brought out of Egypt to die in the wilderness, and they also spoke contemptuously

of the manna which God had provided them, calling it " light bread," and saying, as children often do, that they hated it. For this God sent fiery serpents among them, and multitudes were bitten. These serpents were called fiery, probably, because they appeared very much like bright brass. Whether they were serpents such as usually existed in the wilderness, or whether they were brought upon the Israelites in a miraculous way, we cannot tell, neither is it material. All we know is, that God sent them among the people as a punishment for their transgression, and had it not been for the intercession of Moses, we know not how many might have been destroyed. God heard his prayers

however, and told him to make a brazen serpent, and put it on a pole, so that it could be
seen at a great distance, and then to proclaim
that whoever among the Israelites had been
bitten by the fiery serpents, if they would
only look at the brazen serpents they should
live and not die.   Moses did so; and they
who looked on the brazen serpent recovered.

This incident is very remarkable, because
it is used so beautifully by our Saviour, to
illustrate the benefits of his death, and faith
in him.   In his very important and instructive conversation with Nicodemus, the ruler
of the Jews, who came to him by night, in
the character of an anxious inquirer, our Lord
calls his attention to the great doctrine of faith
in a crucified Redeemer :—" As Moses lifted
up the serpent in the wilderness, even so
must the Son of man be lifted up; that whosoever believeth in him should not perish, but
have eternal life.   For God so loved the
world, that he gave his only-begotten Son, that
whosoever believeth in him should not perish,
but have everlasting life."   John iii. 14—16.

The lesson which our Saviour would teach
us by this allusion to the brazen serpent, is
very justly summed up by an eminent writer
in these words :—" As the brazen serpent
was lifted up on the pole or ensign, so our
Lord Jesus Christ was lifted up on the cross :
as the Israelites were to look at the brazen
serpent, so sinners must look to Christ for

salvation. As God provided no other remedy for the wounded Israelites than this looking, so he has provided no other remedy for sinners than faith in the blood of his dear Son: as he who looked at the brazen serpent was cured and did live, so he that believeth on the Lord Jesus Christ shall not perish, but have everlasting life; as neither the serpent, nor the looking at it, but the invisible power of God healed the people, so neither the cross of Christ, nor his being merely crucified, but the pardon he has bought by his blood, communicated by the powerful energy of his spirit, saves the souls of men." Have we obeyed the call, " Look unto me and be saved:" ": believe in the Lord Jesus Christ." If we have not " how shall we escape if we neglect so great salvation?"

After the incident of the brazen serpent, the journey of the people was continued, and though opposed by Sihon, king of the Amorites, the people were successful, and Sihon was utterly defeated; and they took possession of his land from the river Arnon to a brook which is called in Scripture Jabbok; and for a while they rested quietly in their camp.

CHAPTER XX.

Position of the Israelites at this time.—Balak and Balaam.—The people again numbered.—Moses warned of his death, and his successor appointed.—Defeat of the Midianites.—Request of the tribes of Reuben and Gad granted by Moses.—Men chosen to divide Canaan.

As we are now drawing near to the termination of our history, and as, during most of the volume, we have been going with Moses and the people of Israel through the wilderness, it will be gratifying to our readers to learn that we are now to consider them as having reached one of the last of their encampments previous to the period when they actually entered on the possession of the land of Canaan. After a battle which they had with Og, the king of Bashan, whom they easily overthrew, they quietly encamped on the plains of Moab, on the eastern side of the river Jordan, opposite to the celebrated city of Jericho. These plains of Moab afforded a most delightful place of encampment. They were considerably elevated above the level of the river Jordan, at about eight miles distant, and they had, as their eastern boundary, the high mountainous ridge, called Abarim. Of this mountain, Nebo, Pisgah, and Peor, were only parts; and from their heights there was a noble prospect of the land of Canaan, as it lay towards the west, with its wooded hills, and luxuriant valleys. While they were here, that very interesting incident occurred which is detailed in the twenty-second, twenty-third, and twenty-fourth chapters of the book of Numbers, viz. the story of Balak and Balaam. As, however, this has little to do with the history of Moses, his name not being at all connected with it, we shall be obliged to pass over it in silence, except so far as to quote the remarkable prophecy of Balaam, in which he refers to our blessed Saviour as the "star of Jacob:"—" I shall see him, but not now: I shall behold him, but not nigh: there shall come a star out of Jacob, and a sceptre shall rise out of Israel, and shall smite the corners of Moab, and destroy all the children of Sheth." Numb. xxiv. 18. The whole story of Balaam is worthy of a most serious perusal, as it teaches the awful nature of the sin of covetousness, and the dreadful end of those, who for the love of money will sin against God, and lose their own souls.

There was only one circumstance occurred while the people were here encamped, which disturbed the happiness of Moses, now that he enjoyed the rich satisfaction of having brought them, after forty years of toil and sorrow, so near to the termination of their journeyings. This event was the defection of the people, as they were seduced to licentiousness by the enticements of the daughters of Moab. This was a plan devised by wicked Balaam; and it succeeded so far as to call down a heavy judgment on the guilty; and Moses must have been much pained at heart, when he was compelled, in order to put a stop to the wickedness to have the ringleaders punished with immediate death. In this, and some other things in the sacred history which look like cruelty in Moses, we are to consider him not in the light of a private person, but a magistrate, acting under the express authority and direction of God.

While the people were encamped in the plains of Moab, God directed Moses to have them once more numbered. There appear to have been two reasons for this, one of which is of a very melancholy character; which was, that it might be shown to them how true God had been to his word, when he said that, on account of their rebellions, not one of those who were twenty years old and upwards when they left the land of Egypt, should ever reach the land of Canaan, except Caleb and Joshua. When the numbering was finished we find this record :—" But among these there was not a man of them whom Moses and Aaron the priest numbered, when they numbered the children of Israel in the wilderness of Sinai. For the Lord had said of them, They shall surely die in the wilderness. And there was not left a man of them, save Caleb the son of Jephunneh, and Joshua the son of Nun." Numb. xxvi. 64, 65. The other reason why they were numbered, appears to have been that there might be an equitable distribution of the land of Canaan according to their numbers.

While at this place, also, Moses was directed to march with the people against the Midianites, who were overthrown in a great battle, and utterly destroyed.

When things were perfectly tranquil, the tribes of Reuben and Gad, with half the tribe of Manasseh, made a request of Moses to be permitted to settle in that part of the country called the land of Jazer and Gilead, which being very fine pasture ground was remarkably favourable to the raising of cattle. At first Moses did not seem disposed to grant their request, but rather suspected them of the selfish wish of getting rid of fighting for the land of Canaan, and leaving to their brethren of the other tribes all the toil and danger of the conquest. They succeeded, however, in convincing him that they had no such intention: that they were willing to assist their brethren in the conquest of the land on the western side of Jordan, and then return and enjoy the portion which they requested. On these conditions he granted their petition, and it will be found by all who are acquainted with the history, while they were led by Joshua, that they faithfully fulfilled their contract.

During the period of the encampment on the plains of Moab, every thing was settled in relation to the division and conquest of the land of Canaan: the men were appointed to attend to this duty, and the different portions of the land assigned to each tribe. There was also a great variety of minor regulations entered into, which belonging, as they do, rather to the civil and ecclesiastical history of the Jews, than to the life of Moses, cannot here be noticed.

We have purposely left to the close of this chapter, a circumstance which, in order of time, a little preceded some of the events which have just been mentioned, viz. the warning which Moses received of his approaching death. It will be well recollected by all our readers, that at the time when Moses and Aaron were guilty of the act of disobedience at Meribah-Kadesh which roused against them the anger of God, they were excluded from the land of Canaan; a terrible sentence, but right, because the judge of all the earth did it. In consequence of this sentence, Aaron died, as we have seen, at Mount Hor, in the wilderness. But now that the people were nearly ready to experience the fulfilment of the promise, that as children of

Abraham and Isaac and Jacob they should inherit the land of Canaan, Moses must have felt, without any intimation from God, that his end drew near. But God, whose mercies are mingled with his judgments, saw fit to give him full and explicit warning. We have the relation in the following words :—" And the Lord said unto Moses, Get thee up into this Mount Abarim, and see the land which I have given unto the children of Israel. And when thou hast seen it, thou also shalt be gathered unto thy people, as Aaron thy brother was gathered. For ye rebelled against my commandment in the desert of Zin, in the strife of the congregation, to sanctify me at the water before their eyes : that is the water of Meribah in Kadesh in the wilderness of Zin." Numb. xxvii. 12—14.

It is here that we behold the moral grandeur of the character of Moses. Without repining; without discontent; without any exhibition of fear or distress, he receives the warning from God in the spirit of perfect submission; and as a true lover of his people, and a most firm believer in the faithfulness of God, we only hear him request that a suitable successor might be appointed to conduct the people of God into the land promised to their fathers :—" And Moses spake unto the Lord, saying, Let the Lord, the God of the spirits of all flesh, set a man over the congregation, which may go out before them, and which

R

may lead them out, and which may bring
them in; that the congregation of the Lord
be not as sheep which have no shepherd."
Numb. xxvii. 15—17. This request was immediately complied with:—" And the Lord
said unto Moses, take thee Joshua the son
of Nun, a man in whom is the spirit, and lay
thine hand upon him; and set him before
Eleazer the priest, and before all the congregation; and give him a charge in their sight.
And thou shalt put some of thine honour upon
him, that all the congregation of the children
of Israel may be obedient. And he shall
stand before Eleazar the priest, who shall ask
counsel for him after the judgment of Urim
before the Lord: at his word shall they go
out, and at his word they shall come in, both
he, and all the children of Israel with him,
even all the congregation. And Moses did as
the Lord commanded him: and he took Joshua, and set him before Eleazar the priest,
and before all the congregation: And he laid
his hands upon him, and gave him a charge,
as the Lord commanded by the hand of Moses." Numb. xxvii. 18—23.

It here appears that Joshua, even during
the remainder of the life of Moses, was to
have some share of the authority, and this
no doubt was, that the personal influence of
Moses might be exerted with the people, so
that they might be habituated to consider Joshua as his successor. In one respect only

he was very evidently inferior to Moses.
Moses always had access to the " Most Holy
Place," to consult God as to the course of
conduct he was to pursue; but this privilege
was never granted to Joshua. When he consulted God he had to make application to the
high priest, who asked counsel of the Lord by
the Urim and Thummim. It is for this reason we are well persuaded that Joshua could
not be the " prophet like unto Moses," who
was promised in Deut. xviii. 15; but that we
must look further, even to Jesus the Saviour,
who was truly that successor of Moses, who
will introduce those who believe in him into
" that better country," even the heavenly
Canaan, promised to those who shall be faithful unto death.

CHAPTER XXI.

Moses repeats the laws, with additions.—
Triumphant song after the recapitulation.
—Prophetic benediction.—Moses ascends
Mount Nebo.—Views the promised land
and dies.—Concluding reflections.

WHEN the prophet Isaiah was sent to He-
zekiah, king of Judah, to inform him of his

approaching death, the language he was directed to use was, " set thine house in order." Perhaps no individual upon earth ever set himself more earnestly and perseveringly to have all his work fully accomplished before his death than did Moses.   His own spiritual concerns were already provided for : he had given his heart to God in his early days : he had not left, till warned of his death, all preparation for eternity.   Now he had nothing to do but make his earthly arrangements : to do every thing which it was in his power to accomplish, towards the prosperity of his people, and thus to honour God by the closing labours, as he had by the exemplary devotedness of his life.

In order to this he sets about a repetition of all the laws which had heretofore been delivered to the people : he reduces them all to writing : gives directions as to the times and methods in which they should be kept in the memory of the people.   Besides this he entered into various explanations with the people : he endeavours to humble them by calling their attention to all their past rebellions, and does not spare himself when he speaks of the transaction at Meribah-Kadesh.

In the course of the recapitulation he warns them of the evils of idolatry, and tells them of the terrible consequences which would befall them if they departed from God.   Indeed, if we carefully examine the book of Deuteronomy, there is not one single point upon which we could imagine that Moses could have been more faithful, more affectionate in what he told the people, and what he exhorted them to do. He could have said, just as the apostle Paul did when he parted from the elders at Ephesus, " And now, behold, I know that ye all, among whom 1 have gone preaching the kingdom of God, shall see my face no more. Wherefore I take you to record this day, that I am pure from the blood of all men. For I have not shunned to declare unto you all the counsel of God." Acts xx. 25—27 ; and he could also adopt the language of the same apostle, " For I am now ready to be offered, and the time of my departure is at hand. I have fought a good fight, I have finished my course, I have kept the faith : Henceforth there is laid up for me a crown of righteousness, which the Lord, the righteous Judge, shall give me at that day : and not to me only, but unto all them also that love his appearing." 2 Tim. iv. 6—8.

At the age of one hundred and twenty years, Moses called the people together, and after alluding to his age, in a very touching manner, exhorted them to courage and obedience. He then gave a solemn charge to Joshua, and presented the priests with a copy of the law, directing them most solemnly as to the method of instructing the people. And after this, God gave him a prophetic song

R 2

which he was to repeat to the people. This is so sublime and touching, that we cannot forbear to copy it entire.

" Give ear, O ye heavens, and I will speak; and hear, O earth, the words of my mouth. My doctrine shall drop as the rain, my speech shall distil as the dew, as the small rain upon the tender herb, and as the showers upon the grass: Because I will publish the name of the Lord: ascribe ye greatness unto our God. He is the Rock, his work is perfect: for all his ways are judgment: a God of truth, and without iniquity, just and right is he. They have corrupted themselves, their spot is not the spot of his children; they are a perverse and crooked generation. Do ye thus requite the Lord, O foolish people and unwise? is not he thy father that hath bought thee? hath he not made thee, and established thee? Remember the days of old, consider the years of many generations: ask thy father, and he will show thee; thy elders, and they will tell thee. When the Most High divided to the nations their inheritance, when he separated the sons of Adam, he set the bounds of the people according to the number of the children of Israel. For the Lord's portion is his people; Jacob is the lot of his inheritance. He found him in a desert land, and in the waste howling wilderness; he led him about, he instructed him, he kept him as the apple of his eye. As the eagle stirreth up her nest, fluttereth over her young, spreadeth abroad her wings, taketh them, beareth them on her wings; so the Lord alone did lead him, and there was no strange god with him. He made him ride on the high places of the earth, that he might eat the increase of the fields; and he made him to suck honey out of the rock, and oil out of the flinty rock; butter of kine, and milk of sheep, with fat of lambs, and rams of the breed of Bashan, and goats, with the fat of kidneys of wheat; and thou didst drink the pure blood of the grape. But Jeshurun waxed fat, and kicked: thou art waxen fat, thou art grown thick, thou art covered with fatness; then he forsook God which made him, and lightly esteemed the Rock of his salvation. They provoked him to jealousy with strange gods, with abominations provoked they him to anger. They sacrificed unto devils, not to God; to gods whom they knew not; to new gods that came newly up, whom your fathers feared not. Of the Rock that begat thee thou art unmindful, and hast forgotten God that formed thee. And when the Lord saw it, he abhorred them, because of the provoking of his sons, and of his daughters. And he said, I will hide my face from them, I will see what their end shall be; for they are a very froward generation, children in whom is no faith. They have moved me to jealousy with that which is not God; they have provoked me to anger with their vanities:

and I will move them to jealousy with those which are not a people; I will provoke them to anger with a foolish nation. For a fire is kindled in mine anger, and shall burn unto the lowest hell, and shall consume the earth with her increase, and set on fire the foundations of the mountains. I will heap mischiefs upon them; I will spend mine arrows upon them. They shall be burnt with hunger, and devoured with burning heat, and with bitter destruction: I will also send the teeth of beasts upon them, with the poison of serpents of the dust. The sword without, and terror within, shall destroy both the young man and the virgin, the suckling also with the man of gray hairs. I said, I would scatter them into corners, I would make the remembrance of them to cease from among men: Were it not that I feared the wrath of the enemy, lest their adversaries should behave themselves strangely, and lest they should say, Our hand is high, and the Lord hath not done all this. For they are a nation void of counsel, neither is there any understanding in them. O that they were wise, that they understood this, that they would consider their latter end!

" How should one chase a thousand, and two put ten thousand to flight, except their Rock had sold them, and the Lord had shut them up? For their rock is not as our Rock, even our enemies themselves being judges. For their vine is of the vine of Sodom, and of the fields of Gomorrah : their grapes are grapes of gall, their clusters are bitter : their wine is the poison of dragons, and the cruel venom of asps. Is not this laid up in store with me, and sealed up among my treasures? To me belongeth vengeance, and recompense ; their foot shall slide in due time : for the day of their calamity is at hand, and the things that shall come upon them make haste. For the Lord shall judge his people, and repent himself for his servants, when he seeth that their power is gone, and there is none shut up, or left. And he shall say, where are their gods, their rock in whom they trusted, which did eat the fat of their sacrifices, and drank the wine of their drink offerings? let them rise up and help you, and be your protection. See now that I, even I, am he, and there is no god with me : I kill, and I make alive ; I wound, and I heal : neither is there any that can deliver out of my hand. For I lift up my hand to heaven, and say, I live for ever. If I whet my glittering sword, and mine hand take hold on judgment; I will render vengeance to mine enemies, and will reward them that hate me. I will make mine arrows drunk with blood, and my sword shall devour flesh ; and that with the blood of the slain and of the captives, from the beginning of revenges upon the enemy. Rejoice, O ye nations, with his people : for he will avenge the blood of his servants, and will render ven-

geance to his adversaries, and will be merciful
unto his land, and to his people." Deut. xxxii.
1—43.

Immediately succeeding this, Moses delivered to the people his prophetic blessing.
It pointed out the future history of the various
tribes ; and concluded in these noble and ani-
mating and consoling strains :—" The eternal
God is thy refuge, and underneath are the
everlasting arms : and he shall thrust out the
enemy from before thee ; and shall say, Destroy them. Israel then shall dwell in safety
alone : the fountain of Jacob shall be upon a
land of corn and wine ; also his heavens shall
drop down dew. Happy art thou, O Israel :
who is like unto thee, O people saved by the
Lord, the shield of thy help, and who is the
sword of thy excellency ! and thine enemies
shall be found liars unto thee ; and thou shalt
tread upon their high places." Deut: xxxiii.
27—29.

Thus, we see, that the last days of Moses
were the most active and most happy of his
life : he was bringing that work to a close which
the Lord had appointed him to do ; and though
he knew that as soon as it was finished he was
to die, he made no delays : he went on steadily and firmly, because his sure hope was in
God.

And now came the time when, having
finished his course, he was to enter upon his
reward. The sacred history tells us :—" And

Moses went up from the plains of Moab unto the mountain of Nebo, to the top of Pisgah, that is over against Jericho. And the Lord showed him all the land of Gilead, unto Dan; and all Naphtali, and the land of Ephraim, and Manasseh, and all the land of Judah, unto the utmost sea; and the south, and the plain of the valley of Jericho, the city of palm trees, unto Zoar. And the Lord said unto him, this is the land which I sware unto Abraham, unto Isaac, and unto Jacob, saying, I will give it unto thy seed: I have caused thee to see it with thine eyes, but thou shalt not go over thither. So Moses the servant of the Lord died there in the land of Moab, according to the word of the Lord. And he buried him in a valley in the land of Moab, over against Beth-peor: but no man knoweth of his sepulchre unto this day." Deut. xxxiv. 1—6.

We have now a task to perform which is far more difficult than all the preceding history. We have no funeral sermon to deliver, but we have a few words to offer on the character of him whose history it has been our pleasure thus far to follow. The difficulty of this work, however, is somewhat lessened, because we find it in a measure done to our hand, by one who was far more competent to the task than we can pretend to be; and such extracts as may express our own views and feelings will, in conclusion, be presented to our readers.

" The eulogium or character given of Moses by the Spirit of God, though very concise, is yet full and satisfactory. 'And there arose not a prophet since in Israel like unto Moses, whom Jehovah knew face to face; in all the signs and the wonders which the Lord sent him to do in the land of Egypt, to Pharaoh, and to all his servants, and to all his land; and in all that mighty hand,' (all conquering power and influence) 'and in all the great terror which Moses showed in the sight of all Israel. Moses is called the servant of God, and he has farther this high character, that as a servant, he was faithful to God in all his house.' Heb. iii. 5. He faithfully discharged the trust reposed in him, and totally forgetting himself, and his own secular interest, with that also of his family, he laboured incessantly to promote God's honour and the people's welfare, which, on many occasions, he showed, were dearer to him than his own life. Moses was in every respect a great man; for every virtue that constitutes genuine nobility, was concentrated in him, and fully displayed in his conduct. He always conducted himself as a man conscious of his own integrity, and of the guidance and protection of God, under whose orders he constantly acted. He therefore betrays no confusion in his views, nor indecision in his measures—he was without anxiety, because he was conscious of the rectitude of his motives, and that the cause

which he espoused was the cause of God,
and that his power and faithfulness were
pledged for his support. His courage and
fortitude were unshaken and unconquerable,
because his reliance was unremittingly fixed
on the unchangeableness of Jehovah. He
left Egypt, having an eye to the recompense
of reward in another world; and never lost
sight of this grand object; he was therefore
neither discouraged by difficulties, nor elated
by prosperity. He who in Egypt refused to
be called the son of Pharaoh's daughter, there-
by renouncing the claim he might have had
to the Egyptian throne, was never likely to
be influenced by secular views in the government of the miserable multitudes which he
led out of that country. His renunciation of
the court of Pharaoh and its advantages, was
the amplest proof that he neither sought nor
expected honour or emolument in the wilderness, among a people who had scarcely any
thing but what they received by immediate
miracle from the hand of God.

We cannot fail here to notice the disinterestedness of Moses in reference to his family,
as well as to himself. This is a singular
case: his own tribe, that of Levi, he left
without any earthly possession; and though
to minister to God was the most honourable
employment, yet the Levites could never arise
to any political consequence in Israel. Even
his own sons became blended in the common

S

mass of the Levites, and possessed no kind of distinction among their brethren. Though his confidence in God was ever unshaken, yet he had a life of toil and perpetual distress, occasioned by the ignorance, obstinacy, and baseness of the people over whom he presided; and he died in their service, leaving no other property but his tent behind him. Of the spoils taken in war, we never read of the portion of Moses: he had none, he wanted none, his treasure was in heaven, and where his treasure was, there also was his heart.

The manner in which he bore the sentence of his exclusion from the promised inheritance, is an additional proof of his persuasion of the reality of the invisible world: no testiness, no murmuring, no expatiating on former services; no passionate intreaties to have the sentence reversed, appear in the spirit or conduct of this truly great man. He bowed to the decision of that justice which he knew could not act wrong; and having buried the world, as to himself, he had no earthly attachments; he was obeying the will of God, in leading the people, and therefore, when his master chose to dismiss him from his service, he was content; and saw, without regret or envy, another appointed to his office.

The moral character of Moses is almost immaculate. That he offended Jehovah at the waters of Meribah, there can be no doubt; but in what the offence consisted, commentators and critics are greatly at a loss to ascertain. Had the offence been committed by any ordinary person, it would probably have passed between God and the conscience, without any public reprehension. But Moses was great, and supereminently favoured; and a fault in him derived much of its moral delinquency from these very circumstances. He did not " sanctify the Lord in the sight of the people ;" he did not fully show that God himself was the sole worker : he appeared by his conduct to exhibit himself as an agent indispensably necessary in the promised miraculous supply; and this might have had the most dangerous consequences on the minds of this gross people, had not God thus marked it with his displeasure. This awful lesson to the legislator, taught the people that their help came from God, and not from man ; and that consequently, they must repose their confidence in him alone.

At a distant view, there appears to be very little observable in the death of Moses ; but on a nearer approach, we shall find it to have been the most honourable, I might add, the most glorious, with which any human being was ever favoured. As to his death itself, it is simply said, " he died in the land of Moab —according to the word of the Lord." He was in familiar conversation with his Maker : and while in the act of viewing the land, and receiving the last information relative to it, the ancient covenant with the patriarchs, and the performance of the covenant in putting their posterity in possession of this goodly inheritance, he yielded up the ghost, and suddenly passed from the verge of the earthly, into the heavenly Canaan. Thus without the labour and the delay of passing through the type, he entered at once into the possession of the antitype ; having simply lost the honour of leading the people a little farther, whom, with so much care and solicitude, he had brought thus far.

There is another circumstance in his death which requires particular notice. It is said, " He died—according to the word of the Lord:" the original words signify literally, at (or upon) the mouth of Jehovah ; which one beautifully interprets thus, " by a kiss of the word of Jehovah."

The last circumstance worthy of note is, that God buried him, which is an honour no human being ever received besides himself.

It may be asked how Moses, who was bred up at an idolatrous court, which he did not quit till the fortieth year of his age, got that acquaintance with the true God, which the apostle states him to have had : and that faith by which he realized spiritual and invisible things ; and through which he despised all worldly grandeur and secular emolument !— " By faith," says the apostle, " Moses, when he was come to years, refused to be called the son of Pharaoh's daughter ; choosing rather from God, consult their senses, and depend upon man; and the manner in which Moses and Aaron performed the miracle which God commanded them to do in his name, was such as to confirm them in the carnality of their views, and cause them to depend on an arm of flesh. ' Ye therefore shall not go into the promised land,' said the Lord: and the death of them both was the fullest proof to this people, that it was not by might nor by power, but by the Spirit of the Lord of Hosts, that their enemies were expelled, and that themselves were introduced and established in the promised inheritance. This seems to be the spirit of the whole business: and as Moses had no other end in view but the glory of God, it must have been a supreme satisfaction to his pious soul, that this end was so effectually promoted, though even at the expense of his life.

" At a distant view there appears to be very little observable in the death of Moses; but on a nearer approach, we shall find it to have been the most honourable, I might add, the most glorious, with which any human being was ever favoured. As to his death itself, it is simply said, ' he died in the land of Moab—according to the word of the Lord.' He was, as has already been observed, in familiar conversation with his Maker: and while in the act of viewing the land, and receiving the last information relative to it, the ancient covenant with the patriarchs, and the performance of the covenant in putting their posterity in possession of this goodly inheritance, he yielded up the ghost, and suddenly passed from the verge of the earthly, into the heavenly Canaan.

" The last circumstance worthy of note, is that God buried him, which is an honour no human being ever received besides himself. From the tradition referred to by Saint Jude, verse 9., it appears that Michael, the archangel, was employed on this occasion; that Satan disputed the matter with him, probably wishing the burial place of Moses to be known, that it might become an excitement to superstition and idolatry; but being rebuked by the Lord, he was obliged to give over the contention; and no man knoweth of his sepulchre unto this day.

" Thus end the life and the work of the writer of the Pentateuch, who, by the treasures of wisdom and knowledge which he has amassed in those five books, has enriched the whole civilized earth, and indeed greatly promoted that very civilization. His works, we may justly say, have been a kind of text-book to almost every writer on geology, geography, chronology, astronomy, natural history, ethics, jurisprudence, political economy, theology, poetry, and criticism, from his time to the present day. Books, to which the choicest writers and philosophers in Pagan antiquity, have been deeply indebted; and which were the text-books to all the prophets—books from which the flimsy writers against Divine Revelation, have derived their natural religion, and all their moral excellence:—books written in all the energy and purity of the incomparable language in which they are composed; and finally, books, which for importance of matter, variety of information, dignity of sentiment, accuracy of facts, impartiality, simplicity, and sublimity of narration, tending to improve and ennoble the intellect, and ameliorate the physical and moral condition of man, have never been equalled, and can only be paralleled by the gospel of the Son of God! Fountain of endless mercy, justice, truth, and beneficence! How much are thy gifts and bounties neglected by those who do not read this law; and by those who having read it, are not morally improved by it, and made wise unto salvation!

"It may be asked how Moses, who was bred up at an idolatrous court, which he did not quit till the fortieth year of his age, got that acquaintance with the true God, which the apostle states him to have had: and that faith by which he realized spiritual and invisible things; and through which he despised all worldly grandeur and secular emolument! 'By faith,' says the apostle, 'Moses, when he was come to years, refused to be called the son of Pharaoh's daughter; choosing rather to suffer affliction with the people of God, than to enjoy the pleasures of sin for a season ; esteeming the reproach of Christ greater riches than the treasures in Egypt; for he had respect unto the recompense of the reward.' Heb. xi. 24, &c. This certainly implies a degree of religious knowledge, associated with an experimental acquaintance with divine things, which we can scarcely ever suppose to have been at all the result of an Egyptian education. But we shall cease to be pressed with any difficulty here, when we consider the circumstance of his being providentially nursed by his own mother, under the authority and direction of the Egyptian princess. This gave him the privilege of frequent intercourse with his parents, and others of the Hebrews, who worshipped the true God ; and from them he undoubtedly learned all the great truths of that religion which were taught and practised among the Patriarchs. The circumstance of his Hebrew origin, his exposure on the Nile, his being found and adopted by the daughter of Pharaoh, were facts which could not be concealed, and must have been notorious at the Egyptian court : and when these points are considered, we need not be surprised that he never could be so identified among the Egyptians, as that his Hebrew extraction should be forgotten.

" That the person whom God designed to be the deliverer of his people, should have been a Hebrew by birth, and have retained all his natural attachment to his own people, and yet have been brought up by Pharaoh's daughter, and had all the advantages of a highly finished education, which the circumstances of his own family could not have afforded; is all a master-piece of wisdom in the designs of the divine Providence. Besides, Moses by this education must have been well known, and even popular among the Egyptians; and therefore the subsequent public part he took in behalf of the Hebrews, must have excited the greater attention, and procured him the greater respect, both among the Egyptians and his own people. All these circumstances taken together, show the manifold wisdom and gracious Providence of God.

" On the whole we may remark, that when God calls any person to an extraordinary work, he so orders it in the course of his Providence, that he shall have every qualification necessary for that work. This was the case with Moses :—his Hebrew extraction, the comeliness of his person, his Egyptian education, his natural firmness and constancy of character, all concurred with the influences of the Divine Spirit, to make him in every respect such a person, one among millions, who was every way qualified for the great work which God had given him to do; and who performed it according to the mind of his Maker. Servant of God, well done !"

CPSIA information can be obtained at www.ICGtesting.com
Printed in the USA
BVOW061121120812

297673BV00003B/51/P